PRESI

In the same series

The Right Way to Conduct Meetings
Apt and Amusing Quotations
Right Joke for the Right Occasion
Your Voice: How to Enrich It
Start Your Own Business

PRESENTATIONS

The Right Way to Make
Effective Presentations

J. Stuart Williams

RIGHT WAY

Typeset in 11/12pt Times by Letterpart Ltd., Reigate, Surrey.

Printed and bound in Great Britain by Cox & Wyman Ltd., Reading, Berkshire.

The *Right Way* series is published by Elliot Right Way Books, Brighton Road, Lower Kingswood, Tadworth, Surrey, KT20 6TD, U.K.

Contents

1 Introduction 7
2 How can YOU speak? 11
3 Preparing for success 18
4 Visual aids 29
5 Presenting data 45
6 Confidence building 64
7 Audience control 73
8 'Theatres' of presentation 84
9 Room layout 97
10 Organising a seminar 105
11 Continuous improvement 118
   Index 125

1

Introduction

Effective speaking is a powerful tool to get things done. No matter how clever an idea or impressive a product or service, a potential 'customer' first has to be encouraged to believe in what's on offer. That's where *effective* presentations can often make the difference between success or failure, between winning the opportunity to prove your point or being condemned to frustration.

Effective speaking is essential in any management activity as most managers spend the highest proportion of their time communicating with others – establishing specifications with suppliers, giving instructions, responding to uncertainties, explaining processes, coaching, training and encouraging, negotiating deals and solving problems with others' help. If any of these activities is done inadequately, there is a greater risk of confusion and problems. Consequently, developing the skills which are essential for effective presentations – no matter what the field or situation – is a solid investment in your own future, a defence against frustrations and a promise of greater success.

But there is a price. Away from the familiar day-to-day exchanges with colleagues and cosy conversations with family and friends, many people become uncomfortable in more formal – but, potentially, more significant – presentations. This discomfort saps their natural ability and all too often results in a disappointment – for all concerned – and, for the hapless speaker, a resolve to 'not go through that again'.

But practice is the only sure way to improve in order to succeed and so you must 'go through that again' – and again and again. This book is designed to make the experience less painful; indeed, with growing success, you can look forward to the warm glow of satisfaction that is only achieved by overcoming a challenge.

Fortunately, few people are handicapped by a total inability to speak. The great majority of us have developed natural speaking skills virtually from the cradle and deploy them almost carelessly throughout every day of our lives. But we are all different and it is essential to be honest in recognising our particular strengths and weaknesses in order to exploit the former while not being handicapped by the latter. Chapter two will help you to analyse your own characteristics as a speaker so that you can capitalise upon your natural gifts and can develop into the kind of speaker that *you* want to be.

Effective preparation is the unseen but vital contributor to success in any field. Few indeed are the speakers with the quickness of wit to fashion a genuinely entertaining and useful speech out of nothing. But, with effective preparation, the great majority of us can craft a memorable speech that will stand to our credit. Preparation is a small price to pay for this enhancement of reputation. Chapter three will point the direction to take in preparing for success.

Furthermore, you will rarely have to 'do battle' on your own. In many presentations, at least, few speakers attempt to win their case without the help of various forms of visual aid. However, you should not expect these foot-soldiers to win your battles without your leadership. All too often, 'speakers' drive their visual aids forward so that they all but replace the spoken message. The result is confusion and rout as, without the control of a truly effective speaker, these 'aids' rarely carry the conviction to win the day on their own.

Nevertheless, visual *aids* – if used as such – can play an effective *supportive* role in presentations. Chapter four will help you to keep them in check and to exploit their valuable potential to strengthen your message and to help genuine audience understanding.

Indeed, audience *understanding* is surely vital if they are to be convinced by your message and, without such conviction, your presentation can never be wholly successful. Consequently, how can you best create this understanding and conviction?

Any audience, any individual, will put the greatest trust in his own judgment. You must therefore provide the evidence to enable the audience to agree with your proposals: you must – very often – support your case with figures. But many people are almost as uneasy with interpreting data as they are uncomfortable with the thought of having to speak in public: putting the two together is surely asking for trouble?

Once again, careful preparation can overcome all such concerns and Chapter five will help you to avoid the data traps while strengthening your ability to establish full audience understanding – and conviction.

All too often though, it is not a lack of talent or preparation that inhibits a speaker but a lack of confidence in the face of the occasion. Chapter six considers the most common concerns and fears which often beset a speaker and puts them into perspective. Such concerns are natural – and necessary – for, without them, risks would remain unforeseen and unplanned for. By contrast, using such concerns positively helps to prepare for every eventuality and should lend you the confidence to control any situation to your advantage.

Confidence, indeed, is so often the key to success. When learning to ski, for example, there is an understandable temptation to hold back and to lean uphill – and so you fall over! The trick is to have the confidence to lean downhill. But where do you get the necessary confidence? Chapter six also provides some answers that will at least help to get you 'leaning in the right direction' so that, when standing up to speak, you don't fall over!

So far so good but, so far, everything has been done in private. Identifying the characteristics of good speakers; listing, controlling – and exploiting – our fears; preparation: they are almost academic exercises by comparison with the rigours of having to stand, figuratively at least, in the spotlight; to have to 'perform' under others' critical gaze. What can be done to reduce this challenge?

Chapter seven reviews your weapons. They are surprisingly potent – if used correctly. Starting with the way you stand and move, audiences will begin to form a judgment. Your opening words will immediately add to these first impressions, and the manner in which you address the audience – with consideration and imagination or evident carelessness – will soon result in their conviction – or, in another sense, yours! When 'in the spotlight', everything about you can contribute to – or detract from – your message, and an appreciation of your potential strengths can help you to deploy them to greatest effect.

By this point you will have assembled a powerful armoury of presentation weapons but they cannot be used indiscriminately. Certain situations will strengthen the potency of some weapons while diminishing – or entirely removing – others. When preparing a presentation, therefore, the careful speaker should review the expected 'battleground' in order to deploy the weapons that are appropriate to the circumstances. Chapter eight considers a variety of possible presentation opportunities in order to emphasise the different tactics that you should consider.

Chapter nine also considers the 'battleground' but in the more literal sense of the layout of the room intended for the presentation. If you are in a position to influence the choice of room and its layout, this can contribute to the eventual success of your presentation even before you have uttered a word. A thoughtful choice of room and careful arrangement will help to establish a receptive mood and virtually remove the risk of embarrassing surprises or disruptive delays.

Chapter 10 takes this a stage further in identifying the factors that combine to create a successful seminar. This might be compared with an actor trying his hand at direction, exploiting the understanding of audience reaction developed through experience of speaking, in order to assemble a varied programme of informative and entertaining events. With the forethought and preparation essential for any good presentation, a practised speaker will be able to organise a truly memorable seminar.

And, of course, it doesn't end there. Every opportunity should be taken to improve further, to learn from mistakes and to benefit from a critical appraisal of others. The final chapter suggests possibilities for continuous improvement to achieve fully effective presentations.

2

How Can YOU Speak?

What is an athlete? He might be able to run fast or swim great distances or lift huge weights. (He might also be a she.) But he/she won't be able to do *all* of these things well. The muscular power of a sprinter is inappropriate for a long distance runner and the lissom frame of a high jumper would be unsuitable, surely, for a weight-lifter?

Equally, each 'good speaker' generally relies upon certain well-developed attributes but few, if any, can bring to bear a full range of speaking skills. So, what is a 'good speaker'? What are the characteristics that equip him or her for this unpopular task?

Take a moment to list, in your mind, a number of well-known speakers. Select them from various backgrounds: the media, politics, the stage. Now, considering each in turn, what is it about their speaking ability that is really outstanding? Consider a notorious example: Hitler. To judge by the films of huge rallies, he was certainly effective in whipping up enthusiasm for his cause: his hallmark, as a speaker, was perhaps *passion*?

Come forward several decades and consider media presenters. A friendly and easy manner are frequent requirements, not passion. Yet such presenters are excellent speakers who are able to command attention and to communicate considerable information most effectively. Their hallmark is surely the opposite of the passion seen in military dictators but both – in their own way – are effective speakers.

The point is that there is no magic formula to become a good speaker or presenter. A wide range of characteristics may contribute to speaking success but any individual speaker is inevitably associated with only a limited range of these characteristics.

This personal style surely reflects aspects of the speaker's character and so the choice of speaking skills is not entirely free. Each one of us is born with – or develops – characteristic facets and talents and has to play the best game with the hand that has been dealt. We cannot play an ace if our highest card is a ten – but, at the very least, we should learn to know our cards so that we can play our hand well.

So, in the field of presentations, what are the available 'cards'?

Facets of Good Speaking
As suggested above, there is no universal hierarchy of speaking attributes: rather a 'shopping list' of features that are present to a greater or lesser extent in all speakers. The intention, here, is to establish the list without arranging it into an imagined preferred order. Indeed, there is no correct priority; yes, there is a priority which will be right *for you* but which you will have to 'play' differently according to the circumstances. Consequently, the features listed below are in alphabetical order.

Audience, consideration of the
In spite of not being in priority sequence, it is appropriate that this should head the list for, without an audience, there would be no scope to exploit any speaking skills! However, it is surprising how often consideration of the audience is overlooked even by experienced speakers. This may be apparent in their use of jargon, speed of delivery, complexity of the message or failure to establish a rapport. Any one of these sins – or others – is sufficient to erect a barrier to really effective communication. Consequently, a proper consideration of the audience *must* be present in the make-up of any good speaker.

Body language
This is surely another factor common to all good speakers: the body language may well differ from speaker to speaker but, vitally, it always supports and strengthens the spoken message. However, it is not unusual to see an otherwise good speaker

undermine his own message by ignoring body language. There will be much more on this important subject in Chapter seven.

Confidence
No matter how you may feel, you must try to communicate a feeling of confidence in what you say. Imagine your own reaction to being told by an obviously nervous doctor how he intends to operate on you!

Conviction
This is not unlike confidence in that it is essential for a really effective presentation. However, unlike confidence (which, in honesty, may often be under threat) many speakers fail to communicate conviction even when they themselves are genuinely convinced: they simply fail to express this in their voice and their manner. Such a failing is a severe handicap.

Detail, attention to
This feature, indicated by numerous clues, helps to convince an audience that the subject really matters to the speaker and increases their confidence in both the speaker and the message. Think of the care that an actor puts into vocal expression – or even into a glance. Rehearsals serve to attend to these details so that the eventual performance is a success.

English, command of
This attribute can be something of a two-edged weapon. A fluency and flexibility in the use of words is a real asset as it adds variety to the manner in which ideas are expressed. However, this should not be taken to extremes. While everybody surely recognises the risks of introducing jargon – losing audience attention while they decipher the puzzle that has been set – there is a similar, if lesser, risk in the use of high-flown words and phrases. Your presentation is intended to communicate ideas and knowledge: obscure words – even if they sound impressive – may hamper this aim. Consequently, any good speaker will use language as a most powerful tool but always with the emphasis on *command* and with proper thought for the audience and their real understanding.

Enthusiasm

This is not an option: it is essential. Consider the opposite, having to listen to a speaker who is obviously bored by the subject. How could anybody hope to be inspired? By contrast, enthusiasm can be heard in the voice and seen in the eyes and movements of a good speaker. It is an enormous aid to convincing an audience – even if they do not fully understand your words.

Experience

As in any activity, there is no substitute for experience. And, like publicity, it might be said that there is no such thing as bad experience – providing it is always used constructively. A bad experience while speaking should be seen as a learning opportunity. Why was it bad? What went wrong? How might the problems have been avoided? If you take the trouble to analyse honestly, you will undoubtedly be more successful next time.

Positive experiences – remembered smiles and nods of agreement – add confidence to future performances. You will know that a particular approach has worked well in the past and will recognise the appropriate circumstances for its use.

But, if you lack experience, you must work to make up the deficiency. Prepare more and take every opportunity to practise your developing skills. There is no alternative.

Humour

This can be a useful aid to establishing a rapport with an audience – but it must be used with care and NEVER at the expense of any member of your audience. Treat it like oil on a hinge: just a little removes the stiffness but too much makes a mess.

Integrity

This is another essential if your message is not to be dismissed out of hand. Your audience must be convinced that you believe in your own message. Anything that you do or say which weakens this essential assumption erodes your whole purpose. You cannot, therefore, afford to bluster or bluff your way through a sticky patch. If you do – and the audience recognises this – *everything* that you have said will be called into question.

Knowledge

You would be unwise indeed to attempt to make a presentation on any unfamiliar subject. Your room for manoeuvre would be severely restricted and you would be painfully exposed to any probing questions.

Of course, radio and television interviewers must regularly handle subjects that are largely unfamiliar. But they have, at least, been armed with background knowledge from the work of researchers; furthermore, their role is to draw the greater knowledge from the interviewee. And even this is likely to be far more effective if the interviewer has the knowledge to ask searching questions and to challenge doubtful answers.

Passion

This has already been mentioned as it is undoubtedly a powerful weapon – in the appropriate circumstances. But how often will the circumstances be appropriate? Commitment, certainly, but passion is such a potent medicine that it must be used in small doses.

Preparation

This is so important that the whole of the next chapter has been devoted to it. There is no substitute that can provide the strength in depth of effective preparation so, if you want to make an effective presentation, you *must* prepare effectively.

Voice

A good voice is a valuable asset – but not essential for presentations. If you have been gifted with the voice of a Laurence Olivier, a Richard Burton or a Meryl Streep, it will be a pleasure for any audience to listen to you – but you will not be excused from saying something worthwhile!

Obviously, if you are in the habit of speaking quietly or quickly, you must correct these handicaps by an appropriate consideration of the audience and of the situation. But the

solution to these problems is in your hands; you have not been
condemned without appeal by unkind fate.

Self Assessment: How can YOU speak?
It is not pretended that the above review of the many facets of
good speaking is complete; incisiveness, a friendly manner,
thinking on one's feet are additional and valuable characteristics – and you may well be able to list yet more – but the review
does indicate the variety of features that may contribute to a
good speaker. How many do you possess – or are ready to
develop? Are you prepared to really consider the needs of your
audience? Will you devote the necessary time to preparation?
Can you put enthusiasm and conviction into your voice and yet
speak without gushing like a mountain stream? Do you really
believe in your message and can you convince an audience of
your integrity?

Be honest with yourself and consider your strengths and
weaknesses in the following list. Tick the strengths and put a
cross against the weaknesses before reading further.

Audience, consideration of
Body language, appropriate
Confidence
Conviction
Detail, attention to
English, command of
Enthusiasm
Experience
Humour
Integrity
Knowledge
Passion
Preparation
Voice

Now, returning to the start of this chapter, list a variety of
well-known speakers from several walks of life *who appeal to
you* and, considering each in turn, rate them against the same
table. Of course, you will have to use your imagination in some

cases as you simply will not know, for example, how much they know about a subject or how much time they put into preparation – but what's your perception, your belief?

Once you have completed this for, say, five or six different speakers, review your table and note the common factors – and the gaps. Does *anybody* have a full line of ticks? More importantly, which attributes appear to be most in demand? How do your own ticks line up with these critical features? If there are gaps, what are you prepared to do about them?

Read on.

3

Preparing For Success

Standing up and making a speech is something that few people relish; indeed, most people try hard to avoid it. And yet, potentially, making a speech or presentation can be one of the most effective ways of getting a message across to a large number of people in a relatively short time. In the business world, in particular, it is such a potent weapon that no self respecting company can afford to ignore it.

However, like any potent weapon, it can be dangerous. Used carelessly, it can create exactly the opposite impression from that intended. Consequently, it is essential to do everything to make the presentation as effective and impressive as possible.

A speech or presentation is really a kind of performance and any performance can only make the right impression if it is the result of considerable preparation and rehearsal. The final performance is the visible tip of the iceberg supported by a substantial quantity of invisible but essential preparatory work.

Familiarity with the Topic
The amount of preparation required to give a memorable performance depends upon your familiarity with your chosen topic. The fact that you have been chosen or have volunteered to make the presentation suggests that you will know something of what you will be talking about! But don't be over-confident; don't allow your familiarity to ignore essential preparation. Time spent in thinking about how to explain something may reveal some doubts or uncertainties lurking in your own mind. Question, in particular, the 'knowledge' that is based upon your

experience. Have you interpreted the experience correctly or have restricted circumstances and rash conclusions led you to incorrect generalisations? Take the time to discover and correct these doubts in privacy, not in the embarrassment of a fumbled presentation.

Preparation Time

Even if you have an intimate familiarity with your topic, the minimum amount of time allowed for preparation should be no less than about eight times the planned duration of the talk. This does not include the time which might be required for writing the talk but simply allows for thinking over the way in which the presentation is to be made. How do I start? What's my essential message? Should I use flip charts or slides or any other visual aids? What's the best way to finish?

If, in answer to these questions, you find that you need to carry out further research, prepare overhead acetates or choose 35mm slides, all this is in addition to the factor of eight preparatory time already mentioned.

The Need for Research

If, for example, you were asked to present a case in favour of building an entirely new factory, you would obviously have to arm yourself with a tremendous range of facts and figures. If such a project had been under way for some time, these facts and figures should be available but probably in such quantity that you would be forced to be selective in preparing your presentation. This process of selection would require a thorough review of all available data and this would demand a very considerable time. However, this time would be valuable in increasing your familiarity with the facts and improve your comfort in coping with possible questions.

This is, perhaps, an extreme example which few people will have to encounter. However, even much simpler presentations will be enlivened if specific examples are occasionally introduced to illustrate general principles and such specific examples will demand research; they *must* be accurate.

More prosaically, a welcome speech for a seminar should introduce the other speakers and give their titles. Are you sure you know what they are? If relevant, when were the first products made in your factory? What is the current productivity level? If you are likely to have to quote any such figures – either as part of your talk or in response to questioning – make sure that your figures are factual. Think it through and obtain answers to all the points you need and to any questions that you might expect to be prompted by your talk.

Consideration of the Audience

Although you should now have all the materials available to construct your speech, you're still not in a position to start.

A cardinal mistake which many people make in presenting a speech is that they worry about themselves. What about the long-suffering audience! It is *your* responsibility to get your message over to them and you are unlikely to do this unless you think about them.

This consideration of the audience must start at the preparation stage or else you may prepare entirely the wrong talk. How much does the audience know about your subject? Are they experts or laymen? What do they expect to learn? Will there be any foreigners present with limited English?

Even if everybody can be expected to understand English, will they interpret some of your words correctly if they are unusual in the wider world or, more treacherous, have alternative meanings? What, for example, would you make of the word 'calender'? The immediate interpretation of this *spoken* word in the minds of most people would be the system of recording time or '*calendar*'; only those who regularly work with the machine that presses cloth or paper between rollers would instantly picture this 'calender' without decoding clues from the word's context. And yet, those who have that familiarity would scarcely recognise this as a jargon word. Consequently, you must be particularly alert to identify and remove such traps.

These are important points that must be corrected before you can pitch your address at the right level. If you get it wrong, your talk will either be insultingly over-simple or else the brilliance of your ideas will go unappreciated by an audience floundering out of their depth.

Another important point to clear up at this stage is whether anybody else might steal your thunder. If yours is to be one of a series of talks, you must see to it that you don't repeat the content of an earlier speech or anticipate the content of a later one. However, this important check can be very positive as you can perhaps build on the information given previously. This reinforces the earlier talk and provides a coherent link between the presentations.

The Objective

Once they have heard you, what do you want the audience to *do*? This is the acid test which most talks fail. They have no clear objective or, if they have, many fail to achieve it. Of course, depending upon the circumstances, a talk may be given merely to inform or to entertain but, in many situations, isn't it more likely that you are hoping to influence the audience to *do* something? If, subsequently, they do it, you have succeeded; if not, you have failed!

You will improve your chances of success in this difficult test if you have a clear idea of your objective. So, what is it? Do you want them to *agree* to a proposal, *decide* in favour of a particular option, *buy* something? Notice that all the stressed words are *actions* required of the audience. View the talk's subject from the viewpoint of the audience. How will the audience benefit if they take the recommended action? Arguments expressed in terms that appeal to the audience are far more likely to be successful than arguments which merely appeal to you from your point of view.

The Essential Message

It is unlikely, however, that your audience will rush to 'sign up' as soon as you have finished so you must rely upon them carrying away an essential message and acting upon it later. In many cases, the essential thing to get across is an appropriate feeling – such as confidence, enthusiasm, reliability, honesty. It would be encouraging to believe that the audience will remember most of what you say. But, of course, they won't. At best, an attentive audience listening to a well prepared and well presented speech might manage to recall about 20% of the content.

Consequently, it is essential to make sure that this 20% creates the right impression, strongly features your main message and promotes the intended action.

So what is it? What is your main message? Whatever it is, make sure you get it across to the audience. Keep on coming back to it like the bee to the hive. But, like the bee, vary your approach. Merely mouthing the same words like a parrot will grate. Repeat the same idea but expressed in various ways.

> 'We will fight them on the beaches, we shall fight them on the landing grounds, we shall fight them in the fields and in the streets, we shall fight in the hills; we shall never surrender . . .'

Who would have remembered this if Churchill had simply said: 'They will never win'? Come to that, who would have heard of Churchill?

A Logical Framework and Marshalling Facts

By this stage you should already have the essential outline of your speech. After all, in considering your audience, you will have formed an opinion of their (probable lack of) knowledge of your subject and what they should hope to get from your talk. Also, having developed a clear idea of your essential message, you know where you want to take them. All you now have to do is to plot a logical course between these two points, making use of the facts – or some of them – that your knowledge and research have provided to assist the journey.

Of course, there is an infinite number of ways of moving between two points. The most direct route might appeal to you simply to get the ordeal over but this is likely to demand too great a leap in understanding for your audience. Alternatively, it might be too flat and boring so the audience will lose interest. However, if a more 'picturesque' route is taken, make sure that every deviation really does add something to your central point and does make some progress in understanding.

But which of your numerous facts should you use to assist the journey?

Sorting Ideas

A method that has often been advocated is to jot down all your
ideas as quickly as possible just as they come to you. If you need
any inspiration for these ideas, remember a simple poem by
Kipling which, as a journalist, he always used as a guide.

> **I have six honest serving men;**
> **They taught me all I knew.**
> **Their names are What and Why and When**
> **And Where and How and Who.**

These six basic questions are the very points that you should
address in your talk for, if you don't, they will almost certainly
be raised in questions or, if left unanswered, will leave unsatisfactory gaps in your case.

Having listed your thoughts, you need to sort them into a
sequence that will be understood by the audience. If you find it
helpful, cut your notes into separate points and shuffle them
about like a jigsaw puzzle to see how they might best help the
audience in appreciating your main message.

You'll probably find that some points will have to be discarded and, in thinking about the audience, other points will
have to be presented in a particular sequence in order to be
understood fully. In arranging this sequence, don't forget your
central idea and the need to keep reinforcing it. Picture this
central idea as the spine of a skeleton with each rib carrying
additional information. Move along the spine referring to each
rib or idea as you come to it but showing its relevance to the
spine before moving on to the next rib or idea. In this way, the
audience will never lose sight of your main purpose.

Another way of helping an audience along the road to understanding is to plant signposts along the way. You start by
announcing where you propose to go and then split the route
into smaller segments. At the end of each stage of the journey,
the progress is then summarised and the relevance to the main
theme demonstrated before the route ahead is outlined. Eventually, having arrived at your destination, all the main points are
summarised yet again.

This technique is neatly summed up in the following lines:

'Tell 'em what you're going to tell 'em.
Tell 'em.
Tell 'em what you've told 'em!'

These few lines reflect the essential structure of any formal talk or report: introduction, main body, conclusion. The vital requirement is to present your facts in a logical sequence related to a central theme with an identifiable start and finish.

Starting and Finishing
The importance of the start cannot be over-stressed. It sets the scene for what's to come and either grabs the attention of the audience or, alarmingly quickly, sends them – at least mentally – to sleep.

So DON'T start with something like

'I'd like to talk to you today about . . .'

the audience know this already. Appeal to their self-interest.

'This talk will explain how we can save 15% of our costs and increase sales and market share by as much as 40%.'

They're unlikely to believe such claims but at least they'll listen if only to show you where you've gone wrong!

And, when you've completed your presentation, don't just fade out with a tame

'Well, that's about it – any questions?'

Re-emphasise the benefits on offer and go out on a high note.

'So, if you want to reduce costs, adopt this plan.
If you want to increase sales, adopt this plan.
If you want to thrive in the future, adopt this plan!'

Then sit down.

Visual Aids and 'Props'
Now that the content of your presentation has been decided in some detail, you should consider every possible way of reinforcing your message. An increasing variety of visual aids is available for this purpose but there is a risk that, if used to excess, these will *distract* the attention of the audience rather than assist it. The 'aids' may usurp your presentation to the extent that the audience may remember the colours and patterns without being struck by your main message.

Another risk in using 'aids' is that they provide you with more scope to worry. Will the projector work? Are the overheads in the correct sequence? Will the computer behave? These concerns are hindrances, not aids; consequently, a detailed consideration of the very large subject of visual aids appears in the next chapter.

However, an essential for any well-presented talk is the preparation of suitable notes.

Notes
A really good presentation should give the impression of flowing fluently and spontaneously without emphasising the hours of preparation that you've put in. Consequently,

a talk should never be read . . .

. . . if it is to be an *effective* presentation.

However, it requires some courage and confidence to dispense with the detailed notes that your preparation has provided.

Fortunately, the time that you have already spent in preparing will already have fixed the ideas fairly indelibly in your memory. All that is required is the occasional reminder to prompt the release of all your logical and persuasive arguments. The notes that you use to assist your presentation should therefore consist of just these prompts or cues together with 'stage directions' to use the overhead, lower the lights or refer to an exhibit. Such directions should be emphasised in some way – underlining, alternative colouring, etc. These alternative markings create landmarks in the notes and help you to keep track of where you are.

One of the commonly recommended methods for preparing notes is to put each main point on a postcard. Each point then leaps at you as you move from card to card and, if necessary, there is sufficient room for more detailed information. However, if this method is followed, remember to number the cards or, better still, loosely lace them together to avoid the embarrassment and confusion resulting from getting them out of order.

One remaining risk with the postcard approach is that once you get into your stride you may well get ahead of the cards . . . and then dry up. The problem then is to find where you've got to.

A simple alternative is to use just one A4 sheet with everything on it – underlined and coloured as necessary. With practice, this should be sufficient to see you through presentations of up to half an hour. And after that the audience will be getting fidgety anyway. An example of this approach is shown on the following page where notes that might be used for talking through this chapter can be seen together with some explanations. (However, the 'notes' would not normally appear as a supermarket receipt.)

Use big bold lettering that you can see at a glance even at a distance. This can give you the freedom to move – when necessary – without clutching a sheaf of notes like a precious passport.

Use keywords that will trigger your memory. They needn't be the exact words used in the text and you can use any kind of 'shorthand' – provided you remember what it means!

Segregate the sections using various print sizes or by underlining main section headings.

Make a particular feature of the intended locations for visual aids and, if appropriate, add 'stage directions' such as *WALK TO AUDIENCE* or *PROJECTOR OFF*. Separate such directions clearly by using a different colour or print style.

When you've studied this approach, try doing the same sort of thing yourself using one or more of the other chapters as the subject. This exercise will help to deepen your understanding and strengthen your memory of the chosen chapter while contributing more specifically to your skill at preparing notes. When short of time, it is always pleasing to kill more than one bird at a time!

INTRODUCTION
UNPOPULAR but EFFECTIVE - POTENT
DANGEROUS
PERFORMANCE

PREPARATION
FAMILIARITY v OVER-CONFIDENCE
LURKING DOUBTS?
TIME - X8 (just for the HOWs)

RESEARCH?
SIFT DETAIL (good for ?s)
USE EXAMPLES - ACCURACY!!

AUDIENCE
WHO? HOW MANY? EXPERT? DIVERSE?
JARGON CHECK
OTHER TALKS?

OBJECTIVE
WHAT?
WHY? - AUDIENCE VIEW

ESSENTIAL MESSAGE
LIMITED MEMORY
REPEAT KEY MESSAGE

FRAMEWORK
START + FINISH POINTS (where)
ROUTE?
CONTENT - KIPLING   OH1
SORT IDEAS

SPINE +RIBS
SIGNPOSTS?   OH2
SUMMARISE

START + FINISH (HOW?)

VISUAL AIDS?
AID/DISTRACTION? - PROBLEMS

NOTES
DON'T READ
NOTE CONTENT - KEYWORDS -
PC/A4?

SUMMARY   OH3

Be Prepared! – Summary

Prepare – even if you are thoroughly familiar with the talk's topic – spend at least eight times the intended talk time doing this.

Research. Be scrupulously accurate in any facts and figures: an error will undermine the credibility of the whole talk.

Consider the Audience: number, knowledge, interest, limitations.

Identify Your Objective. What do you want the audience to *do*?

What is your main message? Repeat it in various ways so that even an inattentive audience will recognise and remember it.

Sort Your Ideas and arrange them in a logical framework, understandable and appealing to the audience.

Prepare Start and Finish. Grab attention at the start and go out on a high note.

Visual Aids? Only if they really help THE AUDIENCE – not you!

Prepare Notes – mere prompts for your ideas, not a full script.

4

Visual Aids

A talk that has been well prepared and is well presented should also be well received.

It might even be well understood but, in many cases, understanding can undoubtedly be improved through the *appropriate* use of visual aids.

Unfortunately, too many people tend to use visual aids either to help themselves or as a means of distracting attention from themselves. The 'visual' should be principally an aid to the audience in improving their understanding. Two essential rules should guide the use – or otherwise – of visual aids.

Appropriate visual aids should be used

if they ASSIST the understanding of the audience.

Visual "aids" should NOT be used if they merely

provide you with a crutch or substitute for your notes.

The latter point cannot be stressed too strongly. If visual 'aids' are introduced thoughtlessly or routinely, they cease to be aids: instead, they become hypnotic distractions from your talk.

So, the first thing to decide is when the use of visual aids might be appropriate.

When to Use

Several situations are likely candidates (though not necessarily *demanding* the use of such assistance). Visual aids could be used:

i)   *to advertise* the main points in your talk;

ii)   similarly, *to summarise* and reinforce the main points once they have been made;

iii)   *to illustrate* some item of hardware or physical situation that may be unfamiliar to the audience;

iv)   *to present figures* to ease comparison;

v)   to show *graphical information*; and

vi)   *when interacting* with or involving the audience.

Several forms of visual aid could be used to meet these circumstances but they would not all be equally effective in every situation. The most likely forms of visual aid – all to be discussed at length here – are as follows:

i)   **flip charts**;

ii)   **overheads** (using the simple, conventional acetates);

iii)   **slide shows** (35mm and the computer graphic overhead);

iv)   **videos**;

v)   tangible **exhibits** and demonstrations; and

vi)   **computers.**

Some guide to the appropriateness of these aids in different circumstances is given in the following chart in which an asterisk indicates a likely possibility.

Aid	Situations					
	Ad.	Summary	Picture	Data	Graphs	Interactions
Flip Chart	*	*				*
Overhead	*	*	*	*	*	*
Slides	*	*	*	*	*	
Videos		*	*			
Exhibits			*			
Computers			*	*	*	*

This chart is only a guide. Clearly, flip charts could be used in every situation but, in at least three, the use of overheads or slides is likely to be more effective. Similarly, videos can obviously be used to advertise the main points of your talk but this might risk the talk itself seeming to be something of an anti-climax.

Not surprisingly, the chart emphasises the versatility of the overhead and slides and so explains their frequent use in all manner of presentations. For this reason – if for no other – you should actively consider other types of aid wherever possible.

Because they are rarely used, **exhibits** stimulate audience interest far more than just another slide or overhead. Furthermore, the use of an exhibit often requires a closer approach to the audience and so helps to establish a rapport. Clearly, however, such aids are likely to be limited to relatively small scale presentations.

Apart from this preference for using tangible exhibits wherever practicable, the choice of other aids will be determined by a combination of circumstances and personal preference. However, whatever type of aid you choose, there are some principles that apply generally.

General Principles

i)   Always think about the *audience*: their ability to see the aid and the speed with which they are likely to understand new concepts.

ii) Remember that you want to create an impression of quality consciousness no matter what the subject of your talk may be. Ensure that your aids emphasise this concern.

iii) Your aid will be unfamiliar to the audience. Take the time to describe fully the essentials of each exhibit or aid. Point to each part as you refer to it so the audience keeps with you.

These principles should form the basis of your approach to any of the forms of visual aid discussed in more detail below.

Flip Charts

These can be used with groups of up to 30 in which considerable audience participation is expected. *Training* is the most appropriate situation for this aid. When interacting with the audience, however, the visual aid is prepared 'live' and so, if its eventual appearance is to be meaningful and helpful, some prior thought should have been given to a sensible layout. For example, if you were trying to get the audience to list the pros and cons of a particular proposal, it would be sensible to divide the chart in two so that the number of positive and negative points could be compared at a glance. Also, it would emphasise the difference between the two lists if two colours were used – green for good, red for bad.

This is a simple example of a common sense approach. However, many charts eventually end up looking like meaningless doodles and it's difficult to see how this can help the audience in the way intended.

An interesting variation is to use the flip chart as a base to support numerous adhesive-backed labels of the sort that are used to attach brief notes temporarily to documents. This is of particular value in any exercise requiring audience participation.

Divide the audience into a number of small groups and supply each group with a bundle of the sticky labels. These can then be used either individually or as part of the smaller team to record ideas or thoughts on the matter in question. The labels can subsequently be attached to the flip chart, grouped so as to emphasise the relative support for the various sides of a question.

This approach is particularly valuable in generating audience involvement without seemingly having to 'draw teeth'! However, it does not excuse the presenter from essential planning. Indeed, if the presenter is going to be able to comment constructively on the wide variety of ideas likely to come from this approach, it demands even greater preparation and anticipation.

In addition to planning the layout or format of the chart and thinking about the probable need for several pens, even a 'conventional' use of a flip chart requires some forethought. For example, will the writing be legible at the remotest point of the room? Well rounded letters help in this respect but, in any event, even block capitals should not shrink below a height of about the width of your thumb. The more likely script (normal hand writing) should be still larger and so you should not expect to squeeze more than 40 letters (three or four words) across the width of a sheet.

But will you be able to control the size and distribution of words? If you are to act as 'master of ceremonies' or facilitator in a training session, you will need to focus all your attention on the delegates and not turn away to write. Consequently, there is often an advantage in persuading one of the delegates to act as *scribe*. However, don't exert too much pressure for a 'volunteer' as poor writing will not help your purpose and poor spelling may embarrass your 'helper'.

This risk can be entirely avoided by the prior preparation of **overheads**.

Overheads
The versatility of this form of visual aid justifies its popularity, widespread use and the amount of space that will be devoted to it in this book.

Unlike flip charts, space constraints are unlikely to be a problem and prior preparation can work to create the required quality image. Furthermore, a conventional overhead projector can be used in a normally lit room and can be readily switched on or off as required without interrupting the natural flow of the presentation.

However, in spite of these many advantages, overheads often fail to live up to their potential either through insufficient care in preparation or through thoughtless presentation.

Preparation
These days, with friendly computer drawing software so readily available, there should be no excuse for the scrappy appearance of an overhead. However, even if you do use some such software to help provide that professional touch, you must still *think* about word layout and colouring. Indeed, the very existence of versatile computer 'aids' can seduce you – and your eventual audience – away from concentrating upon your message to the

contemplation of a pretty picture! Even if you avoid this temptation, common mistakes are:

i)   **too many words** for clarity or effect;
ii) **poor word distribution**;
iii) **excessive detail** camouflaging the essentials; and
iv) (less likely now, a lack of or) **thoughtless use of colour**.

Consider each of these faults in turn.

Too Many Words

Never put more on an overhead than you would on a T-shirt!

Unfortunately these days, the ready and widespread availability of overhead projectors has encouraged the practice of transferring quite detailed notes to the projected screen.

Have you ever struggled to listen to one conversation in the midst of two or more? It demands far more of the listener and, eventually, is intensely irritating. And yet, in projecting their notes, this is tantamount to what many speakers frequently do, frustrating both their own aims and their audience!

There are yet more dangers in using too many words on an overhead. You will be tempted to read directly from the screen – losing contact with the audience and almost insulting them with the implication that they cannot read themselves. And of course they will read it anyway. Furthermore, they will read at a different pace from yourself and so, far from reinforcing your spoken message, you will have *created a distraction*.

This mistake may also result from printing a section of a spreadsheet or report as an overhead. Without any concession to the different demands of an overhead, the print size is too small and both figures and words are crammed onto the screen like people at a Cup Final match. Can you see 'little Jimmy' in the crowd? No chance! And the message that you hoped to 'help' will be similarly lost in this clutter. Far from assisting the audience, you will have frustrated and antagonised them. So, for letter size:

> **Your chosen font should be**
>
> **no smaller than this**
>
> **(14 point).**

This advice is important not only for the audience but for you also to be able to read the overhead with ease. When presenting the overhead, it is vital that you maintain contact with the audience by looking in their direction – not at the screen – and so, if you need to be reminded of the overhead content, you should glance down at the projector. But you must be able to do this imperceptibly, without leaning over and without obstructing the view of any in the audience. Consequently, the print must be large enough for you to read at a range of about two metres.

Word Distribution
This can often be inappropriate if you simply let the computer software decide where to split a line.

Entering the words and allowing the computer to move to a new line when there is insufficient space on the current line often results in isolated words and an unattractive word pattern.

A better arrangement of these words only needs a little thought in order to split the sentence into separate phrases that make a more balanced pattern.

What do you think of this

arrangement?

What do you think

of this arrangement?

You should do likewise with the words in your overhead, grouping key words so that they are more likely to be retained as a pattern in the mind's eye.

Excessive Detail
This can be a problem, not only for words, but for over-complex diagrams with arrows in all directions like Custer's Last Stand!

The flowchart on the next page is intended to respond to the size of the audience and the nature of the proposed aid to help *you* in considering options for visual aids but would it be suitable to include in a presentation? Before you start to study it, note the time on your watch.

Well, how long did that take? And yet this is the kind of chart that is often projected for a matter of seconds to many bemused audiences. Is it fair? Is it helpful to ask so much in so little time? Be warned!

Such diagrams are unlikely to *help* the audience without lengthy explanation during your presentation – and yet an overhead should allow you to *reduce* dependence upon the spoken word!

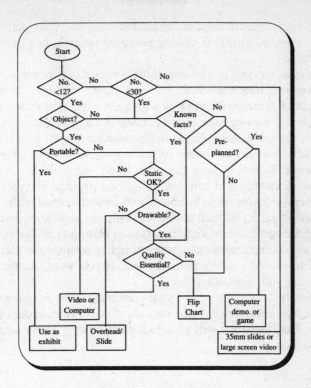

Colour

Colours are much more cheerful than just black lines on a white screen and the careful choice of colour can reinforce essential concepts or ideas. For example, red is internationally associated with 'danger' or 'stop' whereas green indicates safety. These colours could be used to emphasise the contrast between two options.

In diagrams, thought should also be given to achieving a contrast of shade – not just colour – with adjacent colours. This safeguards against the risk of one or two people in the audience being colour blind (a very high probability in an audience of 20-30).

Finding and Filing

Designing just one satisfactory overhead following these

guidelines merely requires some patience but your patience may be tested further if, having prepared several, they become muddled.

A valuable help in avoiding this confusion is to provide each transparent overhead with its own paper backing. Several brands of acetate are supplied with such a backing adhesively attached along one edge so that passage through a photocopier is not disrupted by static. Remove any such backing in advance of the talk to avoid the intrusive tearing sound when with your audience. However, keep the paper in contact with the acetate (static electricity will continue to hold the paper in place). This is essential if you are to be able to make out the detail of the top acetate in a pile; without it, you will only see something resembling the confusion of a multi-exposure photograph! The paper will also prevent adjacent acetates clinging together and may be used to record identity numbers and, if you want, additional notes for your eyes only.

Clearly, as with the rest of your presentation, *preparation* can contribute enormously to the success of your eventual performance. But, there are still pitfalls for the unwary in the *use* of overheads.

Presentation
During the presentation, it is not unusual for:

i)   the **screen to be obscured** by the presenter;
ii) the overhead to be shown for **insufficient time** for the information to be absorbed and understood; or,
iii) the overhead to be left **on the screen too long** – creating a distraction.

As for the preparation of overheads, these points are discussed at greater length below.

Obscuring the Screen
The presenter himself is not the only threat of this irritation. Overhead projectors are reasonably mobile and so are often carried from room to room as required, being placed on a desk or table for use. This is invariably too high as the angled mirror of

the projector often gets in the way of at least some of the audience who then have to crane their necks uncomfortably.

This risk should be foreseen – and avoided – during preparation and room layout. The projector should be positioned lower so that its flat glass plate is no higher than normal desk height. Some projector tables are specifically designed with this feature but simply placing the projector on a chair rather than on a normal table would be acceptable. This at least *reduces* the risk of obscuring the screen and the risk can be entirely overcome by directing the image higher on the screen by adjusting the angled mirror. However, this does then require the screen to 'look down' onto the projector to avoid the distorting 'keyhole' effect.

The presenter is still a threat unless he is constantly aware of his position and is considerate to all the audience. But even this risk can be minimised – to the benefit of the presenter, the audience and the presentation – if a rather unconventional room layout is adopted.

Instead of placing the projector squarely between the audience and the screen, all on the same line and splitting the audience down the middle, consider placing the screen diagonally in one corner. This allows you to maintain 'centre stage' position yourself without obscuring the screen for any of the audience. They merely have to turn their heads slightly for the occasions when an overhead is projected. This is scarcely a discomfort as overheads will not be used in solemn procession (will they?!) but only to emphasise or explain key points.

Timing
Even if the content of an overhead has been simplified to the essentials, it may still contain considerable information which is new to the audience and will require explanation. Make sure that you take the time to explain thoroughly what is being shown. If you do not, you may proceed on the assumption that your audience has understood but, in fact, your continued talk cannot be appreciated because many of the audience are still trying to come to grips with the overhead. They are never likely to catch up again.

Equally, you must not 'sell the punch'. Have you noticed how odd it seems when – on very rare occasions – television news producers project the wrong photograph behind the news presenter? This is such a distraction that great care is taken to ensure that the photograph is screened *exactly* when needed and not a moment sooner. Yet, many presenters project the whole of a detailed overhead slide well before it is even introduced! By the time the content of the slide is mentioned it is stale news as the audience has already read it. Their attention has been encouraged to wander by the speaker!

This problem can be avoided by identifying cue words in your talk. The required acetate can be waiting in place on the projector but this is only switched on *as you mention the cue word*. Furthermore, what is then revealed should only be that part of the overhead for immediate discussion. If there is any more to the overhead, it should be hidden by a sheet of paper (probably the backing paper possibly with your sundry notes).

This not only focuses the audience's attention where you want it but, by reading through the paper on the projector panel, you – and you alone – have an early warning (should you need it) of the rest of the acetate's content and so can introduce it smoothly.

An alternative to this important conceal/reveal technique is to overlay one or more additional overheads on top of the first so that a composite message or picture is progressively assembled.

If you want to point out particular details – perhaps in a chart or diagram – a useful trick is simply to rest a pen or pencil on the acetate on the projector plate with its point on the detail. This totally overcomes the risk of hand shake in using any kind of pointer (particularly the light beam which magnifies any such nervousness) and also encourages you to move away from the projector and to look in the general direction of the audience rather than being seduced by the screen. Proceeding in this way you can be sure that the projected message does indeed *aid* your spoken word.

By contrast, a projected image is so hypnotic to many people that *it should certainly be removed when finished with.*

Once the overhead has been thoroughly explained, remove it to allow the audience to concentrate fully on your talk. If no other overhead is to replace it immediately, switch off the projector and resume your stance at centre stage. However, don't be too pedantic in applying this good practice. If you know that another overhead is due within seconds, the switching off and on of the projector will become an irritating distraction rather than a help to focus audience attention. Think about the reasons behind these generalisations and follow the spirit rather than the letter of the 'rules'.

Slides

A computer graphics slide show that uses a liquid crystal display screen on top of a conventional overhead projector is now a seductive alternative to the simple overhead acetate but, if available, its use should not be automatic. While giving the impression of being keen to exploit the latest technology, graphic slide shows do, currently, have their drawbacks.

The greatest limitation comes from the current need to lower the room lights in order to be able to see the projected images clearly. This virtually condemns the presentation to a procession of overheads with greatly reduced contact between the speaker and the audience. In addition, for those in an audience who have not seen such devices before, they are distractingly impressive – but this may detract from *your* message, not add to it. The audience may well remember the pictures but not the message; the form, not the substance.

However, the LCD panel offers unique advantages for any live demonstration of computer software. Beyond about ten people in the audience, it is not practical to crowd around the computer monitor so either additional monitors must be dotted around the room or, much more powerfully, the computer screen must be projected using an LCD panel. This approach is also helpful for the projection of videos rather than having to rely upon the relatively small screen size of televisions. See Chapter 9 for further advantages of this versatile presentation tool in certain circumstances.

The more established 35mm slide option suffers from the same drawback as the computer graphic slide show in that it demands a darkened room – an inducement for any dozy audience! And, certainly, if a computer graphic slide show is intended, there should be no need for the further complication of a 35mm slide projector. However, if you have photographs of hardware or locations that contribute appreciably to understanding, a slide show 'interlude' – whether 35mm or otherwise –

might well be helpful. In such circumstances, and if you have a choice, the computer graphic option is to be preferred as it is more versatile for the preparation of linking graphic overheads and – as already noted – will avoid the need to scatter additional monitors around the room.

Videos

Videos take over a presentation completely and are usually featured as entities in themselves in a seminar programme. However, videos may also be used in small bursts to amplify a point already made. If a video is to be used in this way, the room must be arranged to be able to show the video at the touch of a button without any furniture removals. Continuing with the spoken presentation after the video should be similarly smooth.

If a longer – or, even, a whole – video is to be used in a seminar, make sure that its quality matches the rest of your efforts. Videos can be relatively expensive to produce and so they often continue to be pressed into service long after their production. But, unfortunately, they do date! This is particularly noticeable if the commentary actually refers to specific dates but even clothing and cars can soon give an impression of living in the past.

Exhibits or Demonstrations

These are very useful to re-awaken flagging audience attention. The reaction is

'What's that?'

Such tangible props clearly demonstrate the existence of something in a way that no overhead or even photograph can match. Even simple exhibits like books lend a sense of authority to a claim or statement. Working exhibits are better still as they arouse the curiosity and interest of the audience. However, thoroughly rehearse any demonstrations beforehand and allow for possible breakdowns or other contingencies.

Involving the audience in any demonstration can be a most effective way of guaranteeing full audience attention as nobody likes to risk public embarrassment. However, make sure that you *don't* cause any embarrassment or you may lose friends! Once again, thorough preparation and rehearsal are essential to anticipate and cope smoothly with possible hitches.

Computers
Using computers in a presentation is just a special form of demonstration and, again, considerable preparation is required. In particular, you should be intimately familiar with the program, its various options and likely behaviour.

Many computer programs are designed to work interactively with the person at the keyboard by posing a series of questions and reacting to the answers. This style of software can often provide opportunities for entertaining, informative and most effective training exercises as they can involve the audience with their own suggested responses. An example of this sort of possibility might be any product design software for which members of the audience contribute their imagined requirements.

As a simple illustration, imagine involving an audience with the design of, say, a roof beam. Responses would certainly be needed for the load to be supported, the unsupported span of the beam and the beam material. Using these responses, the program could then provide a range of options relating to various standard cross-sectional shapes along with cost (or price) indications for each option.

Such an approach clearly demonstrates a company's willingness and ability to respond to specific customer requirements and so, if you use such software, a demonstration of this sort can win strong customer support. However, the approach can be risky as an almost infinite range of results might be expected. Indeed, it is possibly this element of uncertainty that adds a rather wicked appeal for many audiences! Like any potent weapon, it must be used with care.

Choose What Is Right for You
While this review of visual aids has attempted to cover all likely options, it would be wholly inappropriate to try to force every type of aid into every presentation. This would be asking for trouble by over-complicating and fragmenting your performance. For each presentation, therefore, if – after thought – you

believe that suitable aids will help the audience to absorb your message, make sure that you also select the appropriate aid.

This choice does not just depend upon the nature of your presentation or audience but also relates to your own level of experience and confidence. The relative merits of the various aids might well be so close for a particular purpose that the choice will reduce to your own skill and preference. Consequently, search out opportunities to develop confidence with the types of aid that are likely to be of greatest use to *you*.

Do you attend internal meetings to review project progress or for probem solving? If so, practise the use of flipcharts occasionally to assist the group in their investigations and decision making. Do you talk to customers, colleagues or suppliers about your plans, services, products or materials? Such occasions offer you the chance to become adept with overhead techniques in relatively small groups and without the stress that may be generated by a 'big occasion'. Even the taking and, particularly, the editing of home videos can give you valuable audience understanding if you take the trouble to really think about their needs and limitations. Seek out these opportunities and improve through practice.

This survey of visual aids has covered all likely possibilities short of magic and, having prepared thoroughly, your presentation – skilfully made with masterly technique and supported with impressive visual aids – should include a magic all of its own!

Visual Aids – Summary

Only use visual aids to **aid the audience** and not as a substitute for notes.
Decide **which type** of visual aid – flip chart, overhead, slides, video, tangible exhibits or computers – **is most helpful and appropriate**.
Prepare aids to strengthen **a quality image**.
Don't overload any aid with information.
Take the necessary time to explain the content of any aid.

5

Presenting Data

Most talks call for the presentation of data in support of proposals. This need adds to the risks associated with any presentation as handling data poses its own difficulties.

Everybody, surely, has heard – and many probably believe – the cynical comment that:

'There are lies, damned lies – and statistics.'

This probably sums up the unease that many people feel when comparing figures: there is the suspicion in the back of the mind that the presenter is trying to hide something, to con you.

But if you feel this while attempting to interpret others' data, you may also feel there is a risk that any data that *you* present may – unwittingly – contain some flaw which, if spotted, might unravel your whole argument. Perhaps this is why many people would prefer to attempt to make a case without the aid of possibly treacherous figures?

But, if you can take the time to improve your confidence in data handling, you should significantly increase your chances of success in making any business case. And this does not require an understanding of anything more than elementary arithmetic, not statistics! So give it a try!

Meaning
If you were told that the force required to fracture a particular component was in the region of 9 kiloNewtons, would it *mean* anything to you? It would, perhaps, if you were a scientist or

engineer but to the rest of the population this would be no more than a name without a face: there would be no *feeling* for the value. If, however, this same force were translated by saying that such a force would just about manage to lift an average sized car, that immediately creates an understanding which, without the comparison, would have been entirely missing.

This risk of failing to communicate the real meaning of figures is particularly great these days as English speaking populations are divided between those who still think in pounds, inches and degrees Fahrenheit and those who have grown up with the kilograms, litres and such of the metric measurement systems. If you rely entirely on figures, you cannot hope to convey your meaning to all in an audience as their understanding of the measurement units is likely to be so diverse. Consequently, if you are talking to a mixed or non-expert audience, make sure that you flesh out the true significance of your figures with familiar comparisons.

Perspective
If I were to tell you that the FT-SE 100 share price index stood at 3,558 on a particular day, would this mean anything to you? It would if you were a financial analyst or if you owned a considerable number of shares – but to the rest of us? Is it good or is it bad? The bald figure – without essential background knowledge – says nothing.

For this reason, there is little, if any, point in quoting isolated figures as part of your presentation for, while they might impress *you*, they will leave an audience cold and you wondering what it takes to warm such hard hearts! So, if you want to impress or to shock with figures, you must provide a sense of perspective or a standard of comparison for the audience to be able make a judgment.

The 'Financial Times', from which the above figure was taken, included a small graph along with the report that

> 'The FT-SE 100 Index reached an **all-time closing high** of 3,557.7 yesterday, **up 25.3 points** on the session . . .'

I have stressed the words in the quotation which give some

meaning to the figures for the non-financiers. At least we know that we're supposed to be pleased and we have some idea of the relative scale of the movement.

Myopia
But, without specialist knowledge, we still only have a very limited idea of the significance of the figure. If, for example, the figure for the same day the previous year had been 3,400, this would have been an annual rise of just under 5% which, if compared with the annual rise in the cost of living (again using an assumed background knowledge) sounds quite good but hardly stunning.

The important point is that, to impress an audience with figures, you must provide the evidence for *them* to make a judgment. Furthermore, this must provide an adequate history or range of comparison. Simply reporting that, for example, this month's sales are 10% higher than last month's, may again fail to impress if an audience has come to expect monthly sales variation of as much as 50% – both up and down. Whether spoken or not, the understandable reaction will be 'So what!'

Half Truth
Imagine that the sales of a particular product increased by, say, 50% in one month in comparison with the average over the previous 11 months. This could be put over as a significant improvement. But if the product was, say, Easter eggs or ice cream or some other seasonal product, even this longer term comparison might not be so impressive. And even for more 'regular' products, if it was also reported that, even with the 50% increase, we still only captured 1% of the available market, the isolated rise might then be put in the shade.

Consider another possibility where the number of monitored product faults has been consistently falling over the previous 12 months. Wonderful? But *why* have they been falling? If the number has declined simply because product output has also fallen, this is certainly no reason to rejoice!

For this reason, most of our most familiar and most useful measures are ratios. In a car, we can monitor speed in miles *per hour* and, if counting pennies, we would be concerned about

miles *per gallon* (or per litre perhaps). In business terms, an
annual profit of, say, £10,000,000 looks very impressive when
registered on an everyday 'family' scale of values but it would
be pretty dismal for a company employing 100,000 people. This
would give a profit per head of just £100 whereas most healthy
companies would certainly like to see this ratio well into the
thousands.

The important message so far, then, is that isolated figures
will fail to impress unless they are given the correct background
to enable the audience to judge their significance.

Too Many Trees

Unfortunately, in attempting to provide such a background, an
audience is often faced with such a tangle of trees that the scale
of the wood cannot be seen. Indeed, the tangle of figures may be
so impenetrable that even Prince Charming would leave any
imagined Sleeping Beauty to sleep on! So, far from strengthening your case, the thoughtless use of figures might actually
confuse and antagonise your audience.

Even if the number of figures is not excessive, numerical tables
are poor messengers. Consider the following imaginary series.

Jan	Feb	Mar	April	May	June	July	Aug	Sep	Oct	Nov	Dec
85	134	98	117	104	79	155	104	175	124	79	138

Now, cover the figures with your hand and, *without looking
back:*

In what month was the highest figure recorded and what
was it? And what was the average for the year?

If the table had been used in a presentation, it is unlikely to have
been on the screen for more than a few seconds and yet, in this
short time, an audience is often expected to form an impression
of the overall picture, possibly make a judgment of the current
situation and even assess a proposal to influence the future!

And this was just a *simple* table!

Surely, an impression will be conveyed more rapidly – and with
greater accuracy – if the information is presented pictorially? And
this, in effect, is what graphs are designed to do.

Graphs

The following graph presents different data of a series of the same kind as that seen in the earlier table. You appreciate, I'm sure, that you'll be faced with more questions below? But don't study the graph for longer than the earlier table: just form an impression before covering the graph and continuing.

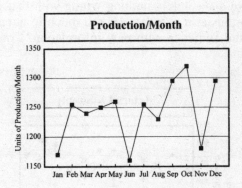

In what month was output lowest?
What was the average monthly output for the year?
And is output tending to increase, fall or stagnate?

I hope that you have a mental image of the graph – including the important values on the vertical axis. Certainly, in showing a graph, these are the things that a presenter will hope that the audience will note because, if they do, they should be able to give reasonable estimates in answer to the above questions even some time after the presentation.

But, if you are the presenter, you should not merely rely upon this hope.
Talk through the graph stressing the messages that you want to convey.
Point out the values on the vertical axis.
Reinforce the picture of the graph.

Graph Pitfalls

One understandable reason for a possible reluctance to use graphs is that many people have been on the receiving end of their ineffective use.

Complexity

The numbers enthusiast, totally familiar with the subject will, understandably, want to share this enthusiasm with the audience. There's absolutely nothing wrong with that of course but this enthusiasm can demand too much in attempting to overload the audience with new information. Consider the following.

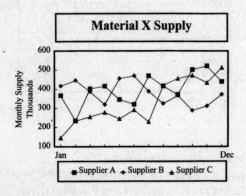

This graph is plagued with several faults but, setting these aside for the moment, can anybody be expected to carry away any strong message from this tangle?

If the lines were in colour, an audience would have a better chance but, in black and white, it would be entirely understandable if many gave up before even starting. The result of this failure might hamper the acceptance of the entire presentation and possibly contribute to taking a poor decision and, no doubt, to the frustration of the presenter.

These unfortunate consequences can all be avoided, as ever, by adequate forethought and by the preparation of a graph – or set of graphs – that will be immediately understandable to even the slowest of audiences.

The key is to simplify each graph so that its message is clear – rather as a schematic diagram establishes the essential principles without a clutter of detail.

To pursue the present example, the speaker's aim is – to judge by the graph's title – to show the relative success of competing suppliers. If this is so, does the audience really need to be troubled by a blow by blow account through the year? Surely, the trend lines will carry the message with more conviction and certainty?

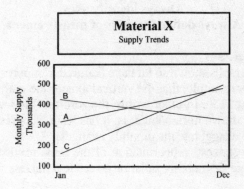

This graph tells the intended story with far greater clarity. Supplier B was dominant in January but his decline has been countered by increasing purchases from A. However, the real success story has been the advance of C from an also-ran to now being the major supplier. What more do you want of this graph?

If you really want to show the detailed variation from month to month, be content with illustrating just one line at a time to avoid the cat's cradle!

But even the above graph suffers from several faults and these should be corrected if you want to overcome fully any lingering audience suspicions. Presenting numerical data graphically should help to convey a strong message but you should do all that you can to ensure that this is your *intended* message.

Anonymous Axes

All too often, the presenter of a graph assumes that the audience will immediately understand what is being represented. Axes may not even be named or, if they are, the units are omitted. This was certainly one of the limitations of the two most recent graphs where the figures on the vertical axis are anonymous. Are the figures units, currency, weight – or what? If you fail to make this clear, there is a danger that at least part of the audience will make the wrong assumption and so receive the wrong message.

Always identify axes.
Always define the units of measurement.

Suppressed Zero

All three graphs shown so far have featured a 'suppressed zero'. Notice, for example, that the vertical axis of the graph on page 49 starts at 1150. In other words, the zero for this scale is well below the drawn horizontal axis: it has been 'suppressed'. The result is to exaggerate the monthly changes.

A more 'honest' representation of the same results is shown below where the monthly variation is seen to be far less significant.

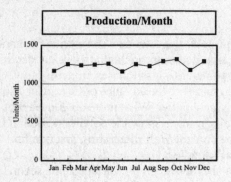

This 'suppressed zero' is highly probable with any computer generated graph as the software will choose a scale to make the fullest use of the graph space. And this, of course, might suit your purpose if you want to emphasise the change – but is it giving a true picture? If you persevere with this 'automatic' choice of axis scale, you should point it out to the audience as this will underline your integrity. If you fail to do so, there will be at least a risk that your motives will be suspected – and so your whole presentation may be undermined.

Muddled Axes
In plotting graphs, the accepted convention is to arrange the axes so that the 'controlled' axis is horizontal and the measured results are plotted vertically. Failure to do this can create some confusing – and misleading – graphs.

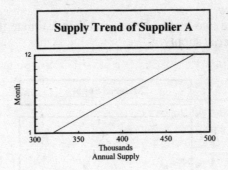

Referring to this graph, in which the axes have been chosen incorrectly, what's your *impression* of the percentage growth of supply from this supplier over the months in question? Don't struggle too hard as you should find the answer more easily from the graph below.

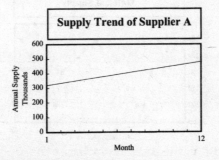

Here, although exactly the same data have been used, the axes have been arranged correctly and the zero has *not* been suppressed. The height of the right end of the line is about half as high again as the height of the left end and so the visual impression given by this graph suggests a growth during the period of about 50%. Was this the sort of figure suggested by the earlier graph?

**If you are not to be
suspected of chicanery,
the picture must reflect the facts.**

Missing Data
Compare the two graphs below and then estimate the average weekly material supply.

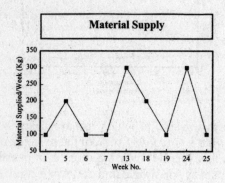

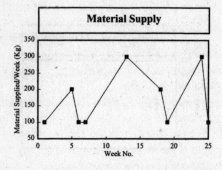

It's rather like a 'Spot the Difference' puzzle isn't it? More-over, neither graph gives an accurate impression of weekly material supply although the second graph is closer to the truth. Note that there are many weeks when no material is supplied at all. This is not at all clear from a quick glance at the first graph as the distance between successive points on the 'Week No.' axis is fixed, although the actual gaps between successive supply vary from just one week to as many as six.

This is a cardinal sin.
The intervals along the horizontal axis MUST be equal.

If there are really weeks when no material is supplied, these 'zero results' should still be recognised. This happens – to some extent – in the second graph by at least ensuring that the steps along the 'Week No.' axis are an even 5 weeks apart and by plotting the graph's points only for those weeks when material is supplied. Nevertheless, even this picture is misleading as the lines joining the points *imply* material supply values for the intermediate weeks so you could be forgiven for estimating weekly supply at about 150 Kg. A much better graph style for this situation is a bar graph – as will be shown later.

What Do You Want to Say?

Here we come to a major hurdle if you want to communicate a message using graphs. Even with just two sets of data, there are often several ways of presenting it – even with a simple line graph. An example of this is shown in the graphs overleaf which all represent progress made during an imaginary journey.

The first graph plots the total distance covered from the start of the journey, recorded and plotted at hourly intervals.

The same data can easily be converted into the cumulative average speed – with successive averages settling down to the overall average of about 50 mph.

Cumulative averages, however, tend to flatten variation (which you may want?) and so the approach to a large city in hours six and seven is masked in the second graph – and all but lost in the top one – but dramatically clear in the final graph in which the average speed *in each specific hour* is plotted.

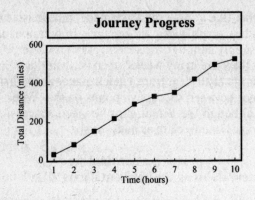

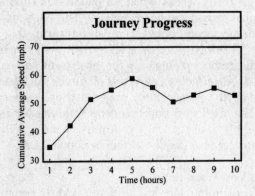

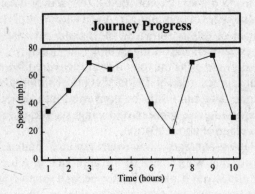

So, what do you want to say? Your choice of graph may help or hinder.

Graph Style
Some mention has already been made of the use of a **bar graph** in certain situations. This style is shown below using the material supply data used for the graphs on page 54. You might agree that it is easier to guess the correct average weekly material supply – 60 Kg – from this style than from either of the earlier line graphs?

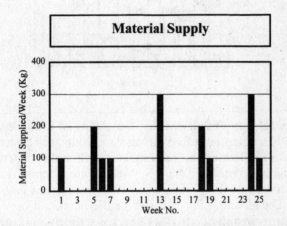

The **line graph** is fine for showing the individual results of one or more *continuous* measures. However, if several measures are to be reported on the same graph, there is a danger of getting a 'cat's cradle' as has already been demonstrated.

The simple **bar graph** is good for *discontinuous* data – as above – but attempts to plot different measures on the same graph soon lose impact due to confusion. Once again, this danger is greatest without colour.

Other graph styles also have their particular applications, strengths and weaknesses and you should at least consider which is the most powerful – and accurate – messenger to carry your information to the audience. Examples and comments are given overleaf.

The **stacked bar graph** is particularly useful to show the contributions of individual components to an overall performance. However, reading the actual values for any individual component is not so easy as for the graph styles seen so far.

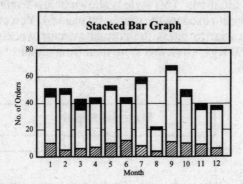

The **3D bar graph** enables the trends in individual performances to be measured directly and compared directly but the data series must be presented in a suitable sequence. In this next example, Black's orders are almost entirely obscured by Stripe's 'defensive wall' for the first half of the year! The situation is corrected for the latter half by when it appears to be appreciated that Black is unlikely to surpass the others' results.

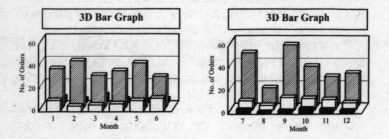

The results with the smallest figures must be the first series.

Other Pictorial Representations of Data

The graphs seen so far have all represented changes with time. But you may want to give a pictorial impression of a situation at a particular moment, a 'snapshot'. One of the most common graphical forms for such a snapshot is a **pie chart** in which a whole 'pie' is cut into variously sized slices as seen below.

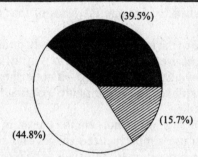

Interestingly, while this form of chart tends to be favoured by sales and marketing personnel, a bar chart representation of the same data is more likely to appeal to scientists and engineers.

As ever, therefore, you should select the approach that is most likely to win over your audience.

Symbols

It is not uncommon to see two numbers compared by means of symbols of different size. This has some real value, particularly if the numbers are large, as anything more than a million is, to most people, just 'very big'! However, if symbols are to be used in this way, they must be scaled appropriately if they are to give a valid – and honest – impression of the comparison. Compare, for example, the sizes of the two squares above.

How much bigger is the larger square?

Surely, most people would mentally try to fit the smaller square into the larger and quickly – and correctly – decide that the larger square is about four times the size of the smaller. But if you were asked to compare the sizes of the 'people', what would you do?

As the shape to the right is twice the height of the other, some presenters might use this comparison to portray a ratio of two. However, this would be misleading – if not dishonest – as most people would still see the larger figure as being four times the *area* of the smaller.

To avoid this risk, if symbols are to be used in this way, it is much better to use similarly sized shapes and simply change their number in proportion to the values to be represented.

The Histogram

If the average weight of an average adult male is, say, 12 stone (or 76 Kg if you prefer), does this mean that *every* adult male is of this weight? Obviously not. But this lack of precision is only 'obvious' because we are all familiar with the variation in size and shape of the people we see around us every day. This familiarity helps us to recognise that adults of either 6 or 20 stone are rare exceptions while still contributing to the overall average. How can this same understanding be conveyed without this daily familiarity with a measure?

A histogram is a very versatile chart that packs considerable information into a simple picture. It is of value to scientists to depict the spread of test results, marketeers for the relative distribution of various types of customer, teachers for examination results, police for illustrating the characteristic perpetrators of various crimes – and for numerous other applications. Consequently, it's worth taking the trouble to understand how to construct a histogram.

Compare the two histograms shown below. Although very

different in appearance, they have both been constructed from the same data to show the distribution of intelligence among a random sample group of 50 people. The reason for the different appearances is that the data have been segregated differently, one giving a very coarse picture and the other much more detailed.

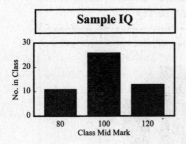
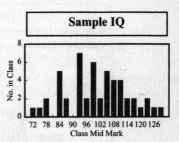

Both histograms indicate the average intelligence quotient to be about 100 and both give some indication of the various probabilities of meeting somebody of either higher or lower intelligence than this average but the coarse chart is too vague while the more detailed chart gives an exaggerated impression of accuracy. After all, the chart is only a representation of the intelligence of this *specific* sample. If another sample had been chosen, a similar pattern would have been expected but it would not have been identical. So, just how finely can the sample be divided before it starts to represent the peculiarities of the specific sample rather than the much larger population as a whole?

A widely accepted guide is Sturgess's Rule which recommends dividing the data into a number of segments given by:

No. of segments = 1+ log (no. of individual measurements)

	Measurements	Segments
To satisfy the earlier promise	0 - 9	4
that this chapter would not	10 - 24	5
involve anything more than	25 - 49	6
simple arithmetic, a simpler	50 - 89	7
guide that will satisfy most	90 -189	8
situations is shown to the right.		

Using this equation for the sample of 50 seen so far would result in the recommendation to split the data into seven classes ranging between the sample minimum of 71 to a sample maximum of 129. Let's say between 70 and 133 for convenience which results in each class occupying a span of 9 to give the histogram shown below.

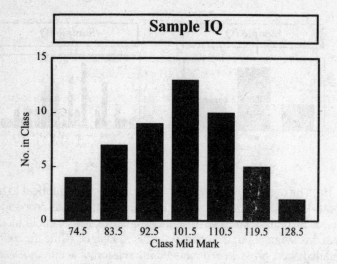

The great benefit of a histogram is that its shape provides a feel for what can reasonably be expected of a particular measure even if, as individuals, we do not have a day-to-day familiarity with it. In other words, we can recognise what is normal and what is abnormal.

This chapter has been but a mere introduction to the use of figures in presentations but, used with care, it should satisfy all of the most common needs and contribute substantially to both the power and clarity of whatever message you want to convey.

Presenting Data – Summary
Well, at least you are now forewarned and so should approach the use of data with appropriate respect! You should also be in a stronger position to avoid being flummoxed by other data

presentations and have the confidence to question critically. In this way, general understanding should be increased and the quality of resulting decisions should be enhanced.

Remember:

Provide **background data** to enable the audience to judge.

Use **meaningful ratios** rather than simple quantity measures.

Avoid complicated tables of data but, if they must be used,
TALK THEM THROUGH and
POINT OUT KEY FIGURES.

Use **appropriate GRAPHS** to paint the picture that most powerfully portrays your **intended message**.

6

Confidence Building

Start with a 'Jog'

What would you think of someone who woke one morning and, without prior training, suddenly decided to run a Marathon? Crazy? Quite: such a trial should only be undertaken after considerable training, starting with far less ambitious distances.

Similar common sense should underline the approach to any unfamiliar activity. Consequently, although you are an experienced speaker – for you surely speak every day – if you are not an experienced *public* speaker, don't be too ambitious to begin with. If you will sooner or later be expected to have to make some kind of presentation, don't wait for the real occasion; go out of your way to seek out opportunities to develop your skills.

Ideally, any such initial outing should resemble something that is not too different from everyday speaking. Little should hang on the outcome so that you do not have to suffer any more stress than is really necessary.

However, depending upon your personality, it may prove difficult to arrange even this seemingly tame exercise. Try standing up and speaking out loud when alone in a room. Clearly, absolutely nothing depends upon how well or badly you may do this but many people will find it a strange experience. And if anybody should happen to surprise you in your soliloquy, how many of you would fall quickly into an embarrassed silence?

However, you may feel that such an exercise is unnatural and so not a fair test. In this case, try telling your partner or a friend what you did at work today. You may be in the habit of doing this already of course but imagine that you have just *two minutes* to describe the important events of the day. Can you do it?

This is a regular test for radio and television presenters and interviewers as they often have to contribute their report in very little time. (The average item on radio or television news occupies only a matter of minutes and even this short time is often divided between from four to seven reports each of about 30 seconds!)

For your own daily news report, unless you think out in advance what you are to say and in what order, the chances are that it will be 'presented' in haphazard fashion and with little coherence. Your thoughts will simply spill out as they occur to you. This doesn't matter in a cosy family atmosphere but, unless you make a conscious effort to improve, you will continue to forgo a ready opportunity to hone your skills for more demanding circumstances.

So how are you going to present the events of the day? In this and in all situations, it helps the memory if you can adopt a neat *pattern*. In this case, for example, an easy and obvious pattern would present events chronologically. However, this might not present the events in the order of importance. Borrowing from the usual radio and television approach, the most significant item is reported first followed by those of progressively lesser importance and often finishing with some amusing titbit. However, in a theatre variety show, the reverse pattern is conventional with the top of the bill appearing last. It doesn't really matter which of these – or any other sequence – that you choose: the important thing is to *think* what you want to do in advance and choose an approach that will have the strongest impact.

Further ideas for ordering your thoughts have been presented in Chapter 3 but don't stick to just one plan: experiment for yourself. But experiment consciously. Be self-critical after each presentation. Did you manage it within the allotted time? Did you cover all that you'd intended to say? Did any subsequent questions reveal a lack of understanding that might have resulted from some failing of yours? Make every effort to learn by your experience and apply that growing experience to improve.

Up the Pace

Relating the events of the day should really be very undemanding: I spoke to so-and-so; such-and-such happened; this could mean that . . . A more taxing task is to try to *explain* some strange concept. Hopefully, you will not have exhausted the patience of your partner after several days of office news; indeed, you may have whetted the appetite for more? In any event, try explaining some feature of your work to your tame audience.

This calls for much more than simply ordering your thoughts: it requires you to imagine yourself *as* your audience. All too often, an inexperienced speaker will thoughtlessly antagonise – and lose – an audience through the careless use of familiar jargon: familiar, that is, to those in the know. You must be constantly on your guard against this sin as it's surprisingly easy to commit.

Once again, as you try this exercise, analyse your performance and attempt to apply the lessons to improve future explanations. Question your friend to confirm understanding and try to understand the reasons for uncertainty.

Criticise Constructively

You *should* be able to benefit from the constructive criticism of a friend or colleague – especially if the latter is also about to make a similar presentation. It would be ideal if two or more speakers could help each other to prepare for an imminent seminar as each speaker would be able to empathise with the others – and learn from observing their fellows.

However, there is an art to criticism and, if this is entirely absent, the attempt may do more harm than good.

It's certainly no help to say 'That's awful. Do it again!' What – specifically – needs to be changed? Was it too fragmented or too quiet, too quick or too lifeless?

Criticism must be specific if it is to be helpful and, preferably, with clear recommendations for improvement. Even then, a detailed, unremitting catalogue of errors is unlikely to help the confidence so a good coach should try to find some good points to sugar the medicine. These should be introduced to counter the damage that an unrelenting list of complaints might do. This approach should help to maintain an effective co-operation resulting in a friendly and continued improvement rather than a sullen plod. Try to make the rehearsals fun and you'll persist longer and improve more surely.

A First Outing
Homely exercises can be very helpful if used creatively to develop essential skills but, being homely, they inevitably lack the pressure of the real thing when you have to stand before a real audience with some real purpose. This adds the nervous dimension that is detested by so many people and you must learn some additional 'tricks' to control the butterflies.

Be Prepared!
Simply, anything that you do by way of preparation should increase your justification for confidence. Research into your subject will arm you with numerous facts – whether you use them or not – but your nerves may not respond to reason and so you must apply a little homespun psychology.

Think Positively
All too often, the inexperienced speaker will imagine all kinds of disasters for the 'big occasion'. This can be valuable to begin with if real precautions are taken against these risks. But if, having taken all possible precautions, the nagging worries persist, they sap whatever confidence you might have had and actually increase the risk of losing control through excessive nervousness.

This danger must be overcome by consciously banning such negative thoughts and replacing them with more positive images. As part of your rehearsals, picture the scene in your mind with you in control. Remind yourself that most, if not all, of the audience know less about your subject than you. You are doing them a favour in sharing your knowledge and there are few other people who are better placed to help them!

This no doubt sounds unfashionably cocky but you needn't be embarrassed as they'll be your private thoughts and, if you repeat them to yourself often enough, you will eventually succeed in increasing a necessary belief in yourself. The result of this personal brain washing will be an improved level of confidence that will be better for you – and better for the audience as you'll do a better job. This satisfactory outcome will more than justify this exercise of conceit.

But even if this trick brings solid benefits during the days before the presentation, it may crumble as the minutes tick away to your start. Of course, this may be no bad thing – in moderation and kept under control. A degree of nervousness is natural and even helpful in giving you an edge that would otherwise be missing. But you clearly don't want to pour yourself into the limelight as a quivering mass of nerves!

Plan the Countdown
Most preparation centres – as it should – on the preparation itself, but there is much to be gained by preparing a schedule or checklist for the time before the presentation or speech. Consider the following as an example.

The Previous Day
By this time the preparation for your presentation should have been completed: you are armed with all the necessary facts (or know where to find them quickly), your notes and various visual aids have been carefully prepared and you have had at least one rehearsal. But have you seen the 'battlefield', the room where the presentation is to be made? There's an old military adage that 'time spent in reconnaissance is never wasted'. This is so because it reduces the risk of nasty surprises in the heat of battle. Nasty surprises can be just as deadly to the presenter, so make sure – if you have the opportunity – that you *study the room* where you are to make the presentation.

Where will you sit before and after your turn? Will you carry your notes, overheads and other exhibits with you or will you have to place them in a safe place in readiness? If the latter, where should they be placed – and when? (The longer they are there, the greater is the risk of someone moving them.)

Imagine being introduced and walking to the spot where you intend to talk. Where will you then place your notes, overheads and such? Is there enough room for everything without risking confusing the used with the unused exhibits? If necessary, obtain an additional table.

Try sitting in the extreme seats to anticipate and avoid audience frustrations. Picture where you intend to stand. Will you obscure any important exhibit for anybody in the audience? Is there a risk of anybody tripping over any trailing cables on the floor? If so, tape them down – along their full length, not merely 'stapled' by adhesive strips.

Where are the light switches? Try them (as they may not all behave consistently). Do you need an assistant for the lights or for a projector? Will the projector work as you expect? If you intend using 35mm slides at any stage, load them and try them all to confirm that they drop reliably, are the right way round and the advance mechanism works correctly. And will any remote control leads interfere with or be disturbed by the audience? Identify and remember the appropriate buttons for operation. Similarly, if you intend showing a video, try it and get to know the equipment. Try to think of everything that might affect your presentation: don't leave it to chance.

If possible, have a full dress rehearsal in the room itself using all the intended equipment and aids. This should remove any lingering uncertainties (although, if yours is to be one of a series of talks, you may feel distinctly odd in doing your piece while others are fussing over theirs).

Rehearsal
Without the benefit of a rehearsal – or two or three – you are unlikely to be able to predict the duration of your talk unless you already have considerable experience. The consequence is that, once started, you soon realise that your planned talk is either too long or too short and you may be tempted to make adjustments 'on the hoof'. Additionally, in struggling to adhere to a half-remembered structure, your mind is working overtime and may falter if thrown off track. Even if you stick to your original plan, a growing discrepancy with the scheduled time may well discomfit you so much that it affects your performance.

And, remember, it *is* a performance that you are giving, not merely putting voice to a string of words. Consciously or not, an audience will receive at least a part of your message from the *way*

in which you talk, your stance, the way you look at them – or don't.
So, in addition to thinking about the ideas and the words that will
wrap them up, you should pay attention to – and even rehearse –
supportive actions. Even more important, you should work to cut
out habitual mannerisms and redundant words that you fail to
notice but which work like the Chinese water torture on an audience – right! – OK! – know what I mean?

Imagine the Presentation
Unfortunately, even well-rehearsed talks do not always run to
plan so you need to consider various scenarios. This should not,
of course, conjure up pictures of confusion and failure! No, the
intention is to anticipate certain possibilities so that, should they
occur, you can switch effortlessly to Plan B. For example, how
will you react to an unexpected question when you're in 'full
flow'? (Read the next chapter.) If the projector bulb fails, do you
know how to switch to or instal a replacement? If somebody
completely rearranges the room, will it matter and, if so, how
will you cope?

   If you think of these possibilities before the event, you greatly
improve your chances of handling the unlikely frustrations of
the day with impressive aplomb.

The Big Day
Start the day with a relaxing shower and take the time to dress
carefully so that you know you look your best. Nerves generate
heat and the resulting perspiration might only add to your discomfort when in the spotlight, so choose what you wear carefully.
Select smart but loose-fitting cotton or wool clothes, not synthetic
materials that impede 'breathing'. Ensure that any collar is not too
tight (but beware of open-necked blouses or dresses as nervousness can often cause a distractingly blotchy skin!). Remove all
unnecessary clutter from pockets – especially coins and keys.

   If you have other work to do before the event, ensure that it is
simple routine and not likely to wind you up – but, equally, it
should not allow idle time to start negative thoughts! If you are
unlucky enough to be programmed immediately after lunch,
keep off the beer or anything else alcoholic – and make yourself
'comfortable' before you enter the presentation room.

The Final Countdown

Focus on the positive and concentrate upon breathing steadily and deeply to calm nerves. When you are finally introduced, gather your notes and so on and stride purposefully forward and then . . .

TAKE THE NECESSARY TIME TO PLACE YOUR NOTES AND AIDS AS INTENDED.

If necessary, clear the clutter of the previous speaker. This simple routine – following your 'match plan' – will get you off to a good start even before you've begun as it will confirm the positive picture that you've worked to develop in your mind's eye. Don't worry about the audience as they will be only too happy to relax and shuffle after the previous speaker.

Start Well

When you are ready, look around the audience and wait for silence.

Ideally, you should have been introduced; if not, introduce yourself – name and title or function – and the subject of your talk and then, without further delay, grab the attention of your audience with your first few sentences – and you're away!

The start is often so crucial to the whole presentation that considerable thought should have been given to it. A good start reinforces confidence and helps enormously with the subsequent speech; a bad start releases those demons of self-doubt that you have kept imprisoned, magnifies your nerves and warns the audience of approaching boredom.

BUT YOU WILL START WELL AND YOU WILL DO WELL – WON'T YOU!

Confidence Building – Summary

Prepare a review of the events of the day to **present at home**.

Explain some concept to a friend.

Learn to criticise constructively.

Research your subject and arm yourself with facts.

Think positively. Convince yourself that you will succeed.

Prepare and **follow a scheduled checklist** for the days approaching your talk.

Get to **know the room**.

Rehearse.

Imagine problems and decide in advance how to respond.

Dress appropriately.

Start well and it will go well.

7

Audience Control

Dressed for the occasion and with a thorough preparation behind you, a familiarity with the room layout and hardware, you have every reason to expect to make a thoroughly professional presentation. So, now the time has come. You and your talk have been introduced to the audience. Take a couple of deep breaths and stride purposefully to centre stage. From now on, you are – or should be – the focus of attention for the audience – unless *you* choose otherwise.

Imagine the audience to be an orchestra and you are the conductor. You must control their attention in order to focus it where *you* need it.

Think for a moment how a conductor performs. Although he has a baton to wave, this would be pointless if he did not also conduct with his eyes – glancing at the featured instrument section; and his body – trying to express the emotion that he wants to draw from the orchestra.

This is what you must do in your presentation. It's not merely a string of words but a performance which should use movement, expression, sound and silence, passion and pathos. If this sounds corny – too bad! If applied, it at least will carry conviction and, without conviction, you are unlikely to convince.

Let's review what weapons you have at your disposal.

Stance
While making a speech, your stance should reinforce the essential impression that you want to create:

'This subject is important, exciting and worthwhile.'

Consequently, a relaxed, slouching stance with hands in pockets is wholly inappropriate. Imagine the news being broadcast by someone lounging back in their chair or leaning, cross-legged against a desk. This sounds incongruous and inappropriate because it is! Casual body language simply does not fit any topic that really matters.

For this reason, you are most unlikely to see any professional presenter using inappropriate body language. Watch them, study them. When sitting at a desk, they invariably sit erect with hands quietly on their notes. If standing, they use a balanced stance, legs about a foot apart and with weight evenly distributed. Their hands are at waist level and may be loosely clasped or, perhaps, holding notes. They are *never* in pockets!

Everything about you, everything that you do, should add to your presentation and not detract from it. The audience should never be given the excuse to let their attention drift.

'I wonder what he's fiddling with in his pocket?'

'What can he see through that window?'

Such distractions should never be introduced and so all such random movements that fail to support your message should be cut out.

This does not mean that you should stand like a big stuffed dummy! Your presentation should give you plenty of opportunities to move naturally and purposefully. Use them.

Of course, depending upon the room layout, you may be forced to stay in one place – either by the presence of a lectern or in order to use an overhead projector or computer keyboard. But, in the absence of these restrictions and provided the room arrangement permits it, some 'wandering' might be helpful. Needless to say, you should not give the audience the uncomfortable impression that they are caged with a hungry lion. Rather, a slow progress will help you to involve everybody and gently dissuade anybody from seeming to be anything but attentive.

Voice

Words are the tools that you use to convey your thoughts and ideas to your audience so make sure that these tools are light and sharp to cut your meaning deeply rather than heavy and dull to club the audience into sullen submission!

You are at particular risk if you can be considered an expert in a subject. Although this may strengthen your confidence and authority, many of the words and abbreviations that, to you, are recognised as old friends may be hazy and unclear to the audience. So make a point of using short, everyday words – even if this requires longer descriptions: better that – and communicate your thoughts – than use more precise but less commonplace words that exclude audience understanding like bouncers at the door of a snooty club.

Whilst seeking every opportunity to convey your message with appropriate words, your voice is your main asset in communicating your feelings. Don't be afraid to use the tremendous range of expression that your voice has. Indeed, *be* afraid of *not* using this range.

One of the reasons for advising against reading a speech is that, except in rare cases, it is likely to come over at a flat, monotonous rhythm that is almost designed to send people to sleep. Talking apparently off the cuff is more likely to be spontaneous and lively with natural vocal expression to match what you're saying. If you want to be convincing, *sound* convinced. If you believe something to be impressive, make it clear in your voice. Be cheerful, be sad, be confiding, be whatever you like but be it with your whole being. Stiff upper lips and dead pan expressions have no place in effective presentation.

Introduce variety in how you speak. Your *pace* should be slower than in everyday one-to-one conversations – particularly if foreigners are in the audience – but don't maintain the same laborious pace throughout. Similarly, where possible, vary the *pitch* of your voice to reflect what you are saying.

Use *rhetorical questions* with the *dramatic pause* to involve the audience:

'What should have happened?' (pause and look around).

The risk of receiving any answer, let alone an unhelpful one, is extremely small as most audiences tend to be coy (except on those occasions when you are giving bad news when such provocation is best avoided). The question does, however, encourage the audience to think.

Above all, *be enthusiastic* with your subject. Enthusiasm – or the lack of it – can be very infectious and its presence can make up for many other deficiencies. The audience is unlikely to be stimulated by your presentation unless you provide the stimulation.

Eyes

To be really effective, any communication should be two-way. Any television or radio broadcast would be a waste of time unless televisions and radios were switched on to receive and people were watching and listening. Audience research is carried out to check this and programmes with poor ratings get short shrift.

In a presentation, you need a more immediate measure of audience reaction. You must use your eyes.

Look at your audience, not over them or through them or out of the window. React to their reactions. Do they have glazed expressions? Are they looking elsewhere? Are they asleep! Respond to these signals by modifying your presentation. This is another reason for not reading your speech. You are not running on rails but can control the direction, speed and presentation of your talk to respond to the needs of the audience.

But you can only do this if you look at them, think about what you see and react appropriately.

Think again of the orchestra conductor. He doesn't focus his entire attention upon the principal violin: his eyes move where and when required to embrace the whole orchestra. You must do likewise.

There may be a temptation to stare at a sympathetic face in the front row – but at the risk of losing the attention of the others in the audience. Moreover, the favoured recipient of your stare may soon feel intimidated and embarrassed and so even they might cease to think about your message. Look at people with warmth and intelligence and don't outstay your welcome! At the risk of mixing metaphors, scan your audience as a shepherd eyes his flock. Attend to strays so that the flock keeps together – and under *your* control!

You can check the power of eye contact on any occasion when you are in a group of people listening to another speaker. If you deliberately do not look at the speaker, you are likely to receive little direct attention. By contrast, if you look at the speaker with an obviously listening attitude you are far more likely to be favoured with the speaker's eye. If you later have to respond, the investment that you have made will be repaid by a far more sympathetic and attentive hearing. Try it.

Facial Expression
While you must use your eyes to establish and to maintain audience contact, you must strengthen that contact by using facial expression that supports and enlivens your spoken meaning. If you ask a rhetorical question, you add significant weight if you, perhaps, purse your lips, wrinkle your brow and stare silently into the distance for a moment or so before beaming as you come up with the answer. Alternatively, you might look questioningly at several members of the audience in turn.

And why not use the occasional smile? This can warm many a message and often wins the reward of some smiles in response. Indeed, this can work both ways. If you see some meaningful expression on the face of anybody in the audience, reflect that expression to show that you recognise and share the feeling. Carried through with sensitivity, this can establish a strong rapport that wins attention for at least several more minutes.

You can test this in any circumstances. Simply look at someone with a particular expression on your face – puzzlement, smiling, dreamy or whatever – and you're sure to obtain a response in no time at all. Beware of macho types though or it might be the wrong response!

Hands
Many people use their hands in everyday conversations in order to emphasise or express their feelings. This is useful as it at least demonstrates a concern about the topic of conversation. Emphasising the points of a speech in this way can be similarly

effective. However, the use of the hands must be *purposeful*.

When rehearsing your presentations, consider the hand expressions that you use naturally. If you are inclined to use the same gesture repeatedly, this is likely to irritate and, eventually, distract an audience. You may not even be aware of this so ask a friend for honest comment. Think about this and make a point of reducing the frequency of such movements. However, introduce alternative gestures by way of variety. But don't be too artificial or theatrical about this or it may erode the sense of integrity that you are seeking to create – and distract your attention.

Balanced, two-handed gestures – the questioning open hands, the 'weighing scales' and so on – are said to be more effective than those made with one hand. It would probably be truer to say that one-handed gestures are more likely to be random and unsupportive of your message. Using the hands – whether one or two – to reinforce or emphasise your message is the important point.

The other obvious use of the hands in a presentation is simply to direct attention to a particular feature. When using the overhead projector, in particular, point to each important aspect in turn and talk it through.

When not using your hands to express or reinforce a concept or for directing attention, don't let them drift back to your pockets or play distractingly with a pen or irrelevant exhibit; loosely clasp your hands in front of you.

Maintaining Attention
Variety is the spice of life and an essential ingredient of an effective presentation. Vary the tone and pitch of your voice, vary your pace, vary your expressions. Introduce visual aids and 'exhibits' to stimulate mild interest. All such methods should help an audience to respond appropriately to your presentation.

But if, in spite of your preparations and your performance, the day has been too long, the lunch too good and people are beginning to nod off: what do you do?

Using your eyes, you will have spotted the threat of a sleepy audience at an early stage. If possible, do something really surprising. Walk toward the principal culprit whilst raising your

voice slightly. This needn't be too offensive; you could camou-
flage your hint with the unspoken suggestion of improving
intimacy or rapport with the whole audience. Alternatively, stop
abruptly, pause for longer than might be expected – and hope
that the sleeper doesn't burst into applause!

Essentially, what you must do is to *involve the audience* in the
presentation so that they have little time to nod off. An old
Chinese saying goes something like:

> **'Tell me and I'll forget.**
> **Show me and I'll remember.**
> **Involve me and I'll *understand*.'**

This ancient wisdom should be the guide for any really effective
presentation. Telling people something can often be boring and
very forgettable; showing something is more interesting while
involving people should guarantee success – or, at least, a wide
awake audience.

But audience participation – valuable though it is – does have
its risks. Reactions can be unexpected and responses unhelpful:
be prepared!

Entertaining

The subject of your talk is undoubtedly very important but, in
many cases, this is no reason to exclude humour. A serious
subject can also be entertaining and is more likely to be appreciated if it is. And remember, you can only expect your audience
to recall a fraction of your spoken message. If you want them to
strengthen their understanding and conviction by subsequently
reading your paper, they are only likely to do this if they have
enjoyed your talk.

It is helpful – and entertaining – to make a point by considering extremes and demonstrating how absurd they often are.
Once principles have been painted in with a broad brush in this
way, finer points can generally be established more easily.

Metaphors are also an amusing way of establishing a point by
showing the similarity between a generally familiar observation
and the point in question. For example, the difficulty of predicting product lifetime is comparable with predicting the life of a

person. There is a statistical probability of a particular value which, on average, will be borne out, but the uncertainty of any specific prediction will be widely understood and accepted.

Games are particularly effective in helping to develop real audience understanding as there's no better way of learning than by doing. This is particularly the case if the subject might otherwise appear very dry to many people. Imagine having to describe the methods and results of some unusual numerical analysis – perhaps of market behaviour or product performance. This would be a real challenge for most people – whether on the giving or the receiving end! But if you can enliven your presentation with examples that involve the audience, they are far more likely to absorb at least the gist of your message.

You might, for example, divide the audience into a number of teams and ask them to devise policies on the basis of the figures and methods presented. This is especially effective if the methods only provide *probable* results rather than certainties as this can excuse 'wrong' answers. The important thing is to ensure that the audience really *thinks* about what they've heard.

Questions

If your well-planned presentation is not to be disrupted, questions should be taken only at the end of your talk: you should try to establish this at the outset. Timing, otherwise, is likely to be thrown completely awry and many questions will anticipate points that you had intended to introduce subsequently in a more logical sequence. Your originally orderly presentation could easily degenerate into a jumble of disjointed ideas.

During the course of your preparation, you may well have discarded several facts because of time constraints or a poor fit with the rest of your talk. These are the very points likely to be picked on by an attentive audience so, once again, your preparation will pay dividends.

By contrast, it is very disconcerting if some bright spark asks a question which you have already answered – or thought that you had. Had he been asleep or couldn't he understand? Obviously, avoid any sign of exasperation; try to be patient and explain the point again from a different standpoint. You may find that others in the audience will also try to help.

If you cannot answer a totally unexpected question, don't try to bluster or flannel your way through as it will detract from the impression of integrity that you have been striving to create. Ask yourself whether you should have known the answer. If, to the best of your knowledge, nobody could be expected to give an answer, say so. Alternatively, if you really should have known, mentally slap your hand, resolve to prepare better next time and promise the questioner to give him the answer as soon as possible after the talk. You will feel a fool but the audience will at least give you points for honesty.

You will occasionally be faced with one or more interruptions. If an answer is due to be given within your planned presentation, say so and stick to your plan. If not, thank the questioner and repeat the question in your own words. This will assist the rest of the audience who may not have heard the question – and it will give you time to think!

Respond as briefly as possible and, certainly, try to avoid a debate. If there is any risk of such a disruption, you must regain control of the presentation as quickly as possible or else the remainder of the audience may become restive. Humour is a very helpful ally in such a situation – but not at the expense of the questioner or you might make matters worse! Acknowledge that the question has opened up a very large subject, express sympathy with any concerns and say that you would welcome discussing the point after the talk – and then continue on your planned course.

Hand-outs

Virtually any presentation which says something worthwhile should be supported by an equivalent report or article. In providing such a report, you largely overcome the risk of misunderstandings which might have developed during the talk and you will avoid having to rely on audience memories to carry your message. Furthermore, if your presentation has been particularly impressive, copies of your report may also be passed to others with recommendations to read it. In this way, your potential audience could be increased beyond those actually present.

Another very significant advantage comes from writing a full report: the effort that goes into organising and presenting the subject on paper is an excellent means of establishing the same logical framework in your mind. You will be able talk with apparently spontaneous ease because you are simply following an already well-used path in your mind.

Although such reports should be available to the audience, they should not be handed out prior to or during your presentation; neither should any other kind of exhibit or reading material. Remember, you and your talk should be the focus of attention with you as the conductor: anything else competes for audience attention and distracts.

Make sure that the written form of your speech is a true reflection of the quality of your presentation and of the quality-conscious image that you want to put over. There is, these days, an insidious and seductive threat to this important aim. Many presenters – unconsciously – sabotage their own efforts with the unspoken message that 'I don't really care about this subject: I can't be bothered to support it with a suitable report.'

This message is unavoidable if, instead of writing a proper report, the presenter merely hands out copies of overhead acetates. Inevitably, this involves a compromise which overloads the acetates while failing to give the information that any proper report should provide. Neither purpose can be adequately served by this compromise. The presenter might offer the excuse of lack of time but, if he cannot find the time for his subject, why should anybody in the audience?

Assuming that you take the time and trouble to write a proper report, ensure that it reflects your view of the importance of the subject. Attend to details of spelling, grammar and layout for they all reflect the extent of your commitment whether you like it or not. Even if the reader may not fully understand your arguments, he will be more inclined to believe them if he cannot spot any obvious – and careless – mistakes.

Audience Control – Summary

Stand without slouching. Reinforce the view that you mean what you say!

Speak with enthusiasm and with appropriate variation of pitch and rhythm.

Look at the audience and react to what you see.

Gesture with hands in support of your message and to direct attention.

Involve and entertain your audience.

Answer questions without waffle – preferably at the end of your talk.

Hand-outs – again at the end – should always reinforce your every message.

Some of the suggestions made here may appear to be pointless fussiness. Nevertheless, everything has been included in the hope that, in using at least some of these techniques, you will demonstrate to your audience that you really *care* for your topic. In showing the audience that their understanding is important to you, they are likely to respond appropriately.

Spare no effort to obtain the response that you want.

8

'Theatres' Of Presentation

When does speaking in public become 'public speaking'? Talking to oneself is supposed to be one of the first signs of madness and so, when talking, most of us are talking to somebody – and so are talking in public. In fact, there's little point in any other kind of talking! So, at what stage is some vague threshold crossed into 'public speaking'?

Two factors are likely to influence the position of this misty threshold: the number of people in your 'audience' and the consequences which hang upon your words. This is conveniently shown as a two dimensional graph – as below.

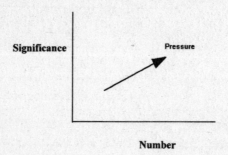

We are most at ease at the bottom left corner of the graph where there are few listeners and little of any consequence is said: a friendly chat in the pub fits this location. However, even in a pub, there is scope for 'public speaking' nerves to be painfully exposed. How would you feel about an entertainer waving a microphone in your face with the plain expectation of you singing the next verse? This would immediately increase the number in your audience and, even though the consequences of your reaction – or performance – would not matter, most people would feel threatened and embarrassed in this situation. This accounts for the abrupt shift into the painful zone to the right of the graph.

Now imagine that, having applied for a new job which really matters to you, you have been called for interview. You face just one person but the consequences of how you present yourself are such that you must work hard to control your nerves. Even speaking to just one person can be 'public speaking' in certain circumstances (in this case moving you straight up the left side of the graph).

Going to the extremes of both axes takes you to the top right of the graph. Thankfully, few of us will ever experience the pressure here as this is the region of statesmen deciding the fate of nations in the glare of world media attention. If you think about that for a moment, it might help to put your more mundane 'public speaking' into a proper perspective!

However, within the field of the graph, there are numerous situations which require public speaking and *each one demands an appropriate response*.

'Small Theatre' Presentations

Most 'public speaking' courses concentrate upon formal occasions with the speaker at least metaphorically on a pedestal while the audience sits in rapt attention. However, most speaking opportunities do not give you the advantage of a pedestal – even metaphorically. Most 'public speaking' – the opportunity to make your case – occurs in small meetings around a table at which everyone is, physically, at the same level. This is certainly likely to be the case for the small scale sales pitch or job interview so what presentation skills can be brought to bear to replace those lost from the 'big event'?

Where to Sit?

An immediate difficulty may be that you have been unable to review, or even to imagine, the room. Consequently, you must be ready to think quickly when introduced. You may, of course, be ushered to a particular seat but, if you have any choice, consider the following points.

Don't take the single chair at the head of the table! (Obvious?)

You don't want to sit squinting into the faces of any of your audience but, equally, you want them to be able to see you as more than a silhouette against the light so, if window lighting is intense, choose a 'neutral corner'.

A corner location is also a good position to choose at any table as you will be able to address the whole of your audience without too much 'tennis twisting' of the neck. Remember from Chapter 7 that it is important to look at your entire audience, not just at one focus of attention. This may be particularly important where you don't know anybody and somebody comes in after the start of your presentation and sits quietly in the background. This may be the real decision maker who has only been able to spare a few minutes from his very heavy schedule, so don't ignore him!

The other side of the coin to ignoring people is to pay them due attention. Take particular care with people's names as they are introduced and take the opportunity to address them by name (and appropriate title if used in the introduction). This small flattery is subtly influential and should at least ensure a sympathetic hearing.

Listen

Hearing – or, rather, listening – is another skill which is special to this presentation theatre. You are unlikley to be wheeled in to say your piece and then shown the door! Rather, your presentation is likely to be the spur for a subsequent discussion where you may also contribute. Such contributions will have a much better chance of influencing a decision in your favour if you have truly *listened* to contributions from around the table and can respond to or build upon them.

Active listening is a surprisingly difficult skill which is worth cultivating. All too often, if somebody else is speaking, the mind is only partly paying attention. This is especially true if, having listened to the initial comments, you think that you have spotted a weakness to be exploited or a chink to prise open. The risk is that your mind will immediately concentrate upon your response and you will stop any pretence at listening.

The correct, if difficult, approach is to make a brief note of the opportunity and then redouble your concentration upon the speaker. If necessary, slow the speaker with a polite interruption to obtain clarification. In spite of the interruption, this might actually be appreciated as it will demonstrate your willingness to listen. Reinforce this impression with supportive body language for the speaker. Look at the speaker and – where appropriate – nod in agreement. Your efforts will be rewarded by creating a good impression, avoiding misunderstanding and by winning the right to your views being listened to in turn.

'Table Manners'

Attentive listening is only one point of etiquette which should win you a fair hearing. Attend, also, to even the smallest points of body language – whether or not you are speaking. If not taking notes, sit erect and lean forward with your hands clasped in front of you. Don't fiddle distractingly with anything and, if you must stare out of the window, at least have a thoughtful expression on your face. Indeed, be careful with facial expressions – especially in a negotiation – as they may betray your thoughts. You are closer to others than in a more conventional stand-up presentation so even the smallest movements may signal your 'real' thoughts – or be interpreted as such. Drumming fingers, pursed or tight lips, eyes raised briefly to the heavens: you have an interpretation of these signals – and so will the speaker.

The Small Scale 'Sales Pitch'

This situation is part way up the left side of the graph on page 84 in a region involving few people but where you feel the consequences – either financial or to your pride – are significant. This is most commonly a face-to-face presentation to a company buyer or group of decision makers or, a situation that we have all experienced, a job interview.

A review of your presentation armoury for this situation will probably tell you that certain weapons are not likely to be available. It's not likely, for example, that you will be allowed to use an overhead projector in your job interview! However, as one door shuts, a window opens. You should be able to define the desires and prejudices of your small audience with greater precision than in a general presentation. In a true selling presentation, you may even know the member(s) of the audience personally and so already have some idea of their susceptibilities. But, even for a job interview or similar situation when you have not previously met your audience, you should have a good feel for their common goal. Plan to show how you can satisfy this need.

Wise advice to any salesman is to '*sell benefits, not things*'. In other words, a customer is not really interested in buying, say, a pumping system: rather, he wants the ability to move his product from A to B as cheaply and reliably as possible. If you convince him that your system will give him this benefit, he'll buy. If not, he won't.

What benefits are likely to be attractive to a prospective employer? Knowledge and ability, certainly, but these have been demonstrated by qualifications listed in your original application and so are likely to be taken for granted. Additional attributes sought at interview are more likely to be enthusiasm, commitment, a personable manner, a sense of purpose and a clear desire to join *this* company. These are more likely to be demonstrated if you have anticipated this interest and *planned to please*.

In particular, you should find out as much as possible about the company and use this knowledge to demonstrate your understanding of the company's aims and problems. Ideally, you should be able to contribute to a solution of their problems. At the very least, you should show that you've thought about them!

Negotiation

The job interview is – or should be – a rather special example of negotiation in which both sides explore a situation in the search for mutual advantage. Numerous books have been written on the subject but the process of negotiation has much in common with making a presentation: it requires preparation, it involves presenting a case and, to an even greater extent, it demands thinking about the 'audience' – the 'other side'.

Negotiation is a big word that is often associated with customer-supplier relationships, industrial relations or, at the highest level, inter-government policy making. But it is important to appreciate that negotiation is an everyday activity that involves everybody both in work and at home. Whether or not we choose to call it 'negotiation', almost any action involving other people requires the give and take that is at the heart of negotiation.

So, the true purpose of negotiation should be a co-operative search for a mutually beneficial position. The result should be a strengthened relationship of mutual trust and dependency – a symbiotic link.

Symbiosis is often seen in the animal world where two totally different species live in close proximity, each gaining from the relationship. Sharks are often pictured with remora fish picking at their gills. The shark benefits by a regular removal of irritating parasites and the remora feed regularly. In this relationship, both would lose if the shark decided to eat the remora.

Why Negotiate?
This is an interesting question which, if answered correctly, will help you to approach any negotiation with a suitable plan. It is a question to be answered not only for yourself but which you should consider from the point of view of the other parties: why should *they* negotiate?

If there is to be any hope of a successful outcome, all parties involved must recognise the importance of three key conditions.

1. Everybody must recognise a **need** to be satisfied. If there is not a general recognition of the need, there is unlikely to be a genuine attempt to negotiate.
2. All sides must **want** to reach agreement.
3. Each party to the negotiation must have the power and responsibility to be **flexible**.

Be Prepared!
Yes, it's that motto again! This should be the first sensible move for any negotiation. You have a better chance of

persuading others of the benefits of your proposals if you present your plans imaginatively and with conviction. But, even more than in any other type of presentation, in a negotiation, you want your audience to *do* something. Consequently, you must try hard to picture the situation from their point of view. What are *their* interests? How might your proposals benefit *them*? What might they lose and how might such losses be eased?

If you want to convince somebody of the justice of your position, it is vital that *they believe* that you have taken their position into account. If you can anticipate the concerns from the other side, you can prepare responses in advance.

But don't over-prepare! A negotiation should be an exploratory process of give and take requiring creative and imaginative thinking. If you come to the negotiating table with a case prepared in great detail to the umpteenth decimal point, you will be unlikely to listen properly to any alternatives which would sacrifice all your hard work. Others will quickly note your stubbornness and the negotiation will deteriorate to mutually destructive fighting.

Instead, therefore, of developing your chosen plan in great detail, prepare a variety of positions in broad brush terms responding to imaginative 'what if' questions. Certainly, you should prepare to present your favoured option as convincingly as possible but you should not allow this to blind you to other possibilities.

If you are to negotiate as part of a team, decide who is to do what and agree your opening position and room for manoeuvre limited by an agreed fall-back position.

Your Place or Mine?

The apparently mundane aspects of preparation should be established in greater detail. Why (the purpose), what (the agenda), where, when, who is to attend and how long any meeting should last must be clearly established if the negotiation is to get off on the right foot. If you are to host the meeting, give careful thought to room arrangements as they can influence the tone of the meeting. This is a surprisingly large topic in itself and so will be dealt with in the next chapter.

Breaking the Ice

People will only co-operate fully and freely if they trust one another. So, to improve the chances of obtaining a mutually beneficial agreement from negotiation, it is worth working at developing this trust. Of course, previous associations might already have done this – or destroyed trust for ever – but anything you do to improve trust will ease the path of negotiation.

To this end, it is worth starting any negotiation with an appropriate period of small talk so that all present have the chance to establish their credentials at least at a personal level. At the very least, if any people have travelled any distance, they should be offered some refreshment before getting down to business.

Procedure

Agreeing the procedure of the meeting should be an easing-in to the process of negotiation. Get into the habit of agreeing so, even if the agenda, purpose and duration of the meeting have been previously established in writing, start the meeting by re-affirming them with an agreement. This also sets a pace for the meeting and moves all conversations firmly from small talk to the business of the day.

Opening Statements

The agenda should provide all parties to the negotiation with the chance to present their opening positions. During this time, others should *concentrate on listening* attentively, interrupting only to clarify and to improve understanding, not to challenge. This need to listen is more than usually important as it provides an opportunity to learn and to understand the others' needs without having to continue to rely upon your own imagination of their position.

Opening statements or presentations should establish your own position in broad terms without spelling out any assumptions about others' positions or imagined joint interests. Such assumptions might irritate and set up barriers to progress. Great care should have gone into preparing a clear presentation of your position as briefly as possible in order to bring the others into the negotiation without frustrating delay. This courtesy of brevity should be appreciated and reciprocated by experienced negotiators and contributes to the mutual respect required for successful negotiation.

After each opening statement, there should be an opportunity for others to question – for clarification – and to summarise their understanding of the statement. Words are imperfect means of carrying ideas and, while each presenter will have attempted to express himself clearly, there is always the possibility of misunderstanding which, if not cleared up immediately, may stand in the way of an eventual agreement.

Exploration

This is the nub of negotiation where you will either progress to a mutually beneficial agreement or slip back into recrimination. In essence, this is rather like brainstorming in which ideas should be voiced and explored without criticism in the search for mutual advantage. Every effort should go into building the right environment for this search. If you feel inclined to challenge aggressively, bite your tongue but take every opportunity to maintain – or, even, to enhance – the other's self-esteem.

If all contribute in the right spirit to this exploration, the exchange of ideas should slowly shape a joint recognition of common interest and the outline for an agreement. Inevitably, each party must be prepared to move from his initial position and there must be a responsive give and take to encourage such movement.

Review and summarise points of agreement as you proceed so as to reward and recognise the progress and to renew attention on remaining points at issue.

Agreement

If the negotiation has been conducted in a constructive and cordial atmosphere to this point, there can be every expectation that the momentum will be sustained to hammer out a final agreement with all the necessary hard bargaining that might be involved for any commercial or resource questions. This is so because all parties will, by this point, recognise that they have much to gain from a successful conclusion and much to lose from a failure to agree.

However, this phase of negotiation requires particular care to be clear in establishing a joint understanding of the agreement with every 'i' dotted and every 't' crossed. For example, what should happen in the event of any party failing to keep to the agreement? There are bound to be circumstances which would force this result and it would help to recognise and to deal with them in advance to minimise the damage to future relations.

Closing the Deal
A final re-statement of the agreement, to close the meeting, should remove any chance of subsequent friction through misunderstanding. For any formal negotiation or decision-making meeting, this should be quickly followed by a written agreement or minutes which reflect the agreement without distortion, subsequent additions, omissions or favouritism. The written agreement should confirm the trust established by the meeting.

Negotiating in this way will help to remove uncertainty and build a more secure future for all concerned.

'Large Theatre' Presentations
This is the more usual understanding of 'public speaking' at which most of the techniques reviewed in any course can be fully exploited – body language, visual aids, audience control, etc. But if the presentation is to be even more challenging than a simple communication exercise, yet more preparation will pay dividends.

You may, for example, have to convey bad news to an audience which can be expected to be anything but sympathetic. This raises the stakes and shifts the point in the earlier graph toward the dizzy – and uncomfortable – heights of world statesmen! Aggressive interruptions can now be expected and will require a cool nerve and quick thinking to remain in control.

Don't beat about the bush: get any bad news over with clearly and quickly in order to focus, as soon as possible, on any silver lining that you can foresee. There must *always* be a silver lining!

You can give yourself a valuable – and, possibly – decisive edge if you have imagined in advance all the possible reactions, questions and comments of your audience. This, of course, is easier said than done and, even if your imagination is up to it, your answers may not be! Nevertheless, the effort improves your chances of at least controlling the meeting, if not winning many friends.

What are you planning to do about it? Who will be affected? When will it happen? How will the Company respond? Why has this happened? Where did the business go?

Call up Kipling's 'six honest serving men' to help you list the questions to be expected and prepare answers for them all – even if they are not what you would like to say.

Media Interviews

These are, potentially, even more risky and, realising this, most companies require their employees to channel all requests for media interviews on thorny subjects to the Company experts. However, not all media interviews need be so threatening and so almost anybody might be button-holed for a 'good news' interview following, say, a giant order or the winning of an award.

But even with seemingly benign events, it's worth taking the trouble to prepare what you want to say in advance. In agreeing to an interview, you are already sacrificing a large measure of control to the interviewer and he may have very different intentions from yours! For this reason, you must first decide on the likely purpose of the interviewer. If you are to be little more than a live 'exhibit' to help announce some local event, then the interviewer will surely be helpful in order to bring out the key details – what, where, when, how much, how long and so on – as efficiently as possible.

By contrast, if the topic is in any way controversial, you should expect the interviewer to probe critically as though representing the other side of the question. You should not resent this but see it as an opportunity to put over your case as strongly as you can, knowing that the interviewer will attempt to balance the score.

Try to anticipate the questions that the interviewer might be expected to ask. Prepare answers to these imagined questions which allow you to get over your viewpoint as clearly as possible. However, if the interview is to be televised, your preparation must be consigned to your memory and not to notes as frequent glances away from the questioner will dilute your own integrity in the eyes of many viewers. You must make a point of looking into the eyes of your questioner. This is easily done if you are in the same location as the interviewer but if you are in a remote studio the interviewer's eyes are, in effect, the camera's lens so you must look steadfastly in that direction.

If you later congratulate yourself on giving a fine interview, wait for the broadcast or the publication of the article! Once again, 'Be Prepared' is an excellent motto!

Training
Returning from the graph's painful zone, training should be far less stressful as the majority – if not all – delegates and presenters involved in training *want* to be there and so you start with an enormous advantage. However, in spite of its positive aims, training is an exception to normal daily life and so may be seen as threatening. Indeed, if formal education was the last memory of 'training', a distinctly cool attitude might be expected. So, make it fun! Try to make the learning enjoyable and it will be more successful – for everybody.

The training programme should alternate between short lectures and opportunities to put the new knowledge into practice. Beyond that, you should limit the amount that the delegates are expected to absorb in any session.

The only drawback peculiar to this 'theatre' of presentation is that timing can be difficult to predict and to control on the day. However, in a day's programme, there always should be sufficient flexibility to respond to the needs of the delegates while hoping that the 'swings and roundabouts' of several sessions will bring the day to a close more or less on time.

Summary
There are numerous opportunities to use various presentation skills every day but you must learn to exploit the skills that are most appropriate:

In small scale meetings, **choose where to sit with care**.
In all circumstances requiring an exchange of views, **listen**

with care and attention in order to win the right to be heard – and listened to – in turn.

Emphasise your attentiveness using **supportive body language**.

When attempting to persuade, **stress those features that will benefit your audience**.

When negotiating:

> Prepare in advance – but not in too much detail:
> rather, consider various scenarios.
> Attend to the important details of time, place and agreed procedure.
> Be brief with opening statements.
> Interrupt for clarification and improved understanding.
> Explore options imaginatively for mutual benefit.
> Spell out in the final agreement how to deal with possible problems.

For bad news, get it over quickly
and try to **anticipate and prepare answers for questions**.

Try to **anticipate questions for media interviews** also.
Keep cool but don't allow the interviewer to control the exchange entirely.
Put your point of view over clearly and with conviction.

For training, involve the delegates. Intersperse lectures with exercises for the new skills or knowledge and **make it fun!**

9

Room Layout

If you are responsible for room layout – whether for a formal presentation or for any kind of meeting – you should appreciate that you have a probably significant influence over the opening tone for the occasion. Imagine, for example, the thought that goes into establishing the seating plan at any wedding so that egos are satisfied and conversations contribute to the great day.

In much the same way, the chosen room and seating plan can contribute to – or detract from – any event involving several people.

As presenter, you want to remain in control and preparation is vital. Laying out the room to suit your purpose is one practical aspect of such preparation.

Why Meet?

You want the occasion – seminar, training session, meeting – to be a success so you should express this wish with the care used in selecting and organising the room. Room layout should be heavily influenced by the purpose of the meeting as what will assist one objective will hinder another. So, what's the *purpose* of your meeting: a face-to-face exchange, a routine committee meeting, a problem solving group, training seminar or customer presentation?

Face-to-Face Meetings

This is firmly in the realm of 'small theatre' and so you are likely to choose to meet in an office, possibly your own. Even so, you should not ignore the unspoken message of the seating arrangement. If you remain behind the desk while anybody else sits on a chair, with or without a table, you immediately give yourself a position of influence. If, therefore, you want to establish a more balanced relationship, choosing to abandon the desk in favour of one of the other chairs may help to create the right impression.

Larger Meetings

Moving out of your normal office, you have a much wider range of options to suit the purpose of the meeting or presentation. You should obviously consider the number of people likely to attend and select a meeting room of *suitable size*. This must clearly be big enough to seat all those expected but not so large that they 'rattle around', giving the impression that many people haven't bothered to turn up; this would start the meeting badly.

Also, consider the *quality of the room* to reflect your hopes for the meeting. If the room and its furnishings are down at heel, this betrays a careless attitude to those attending and, again, sets the wrong tone. By contrast, if the chosen room has a proper business-like aura, it will encourage a committed, responsible approach in all those attending.

The atmosphere of the room may well be every bit as important in the literal sense. If the occasion is expected to attract or require a high attendance, the total body heat of those present will, without adequate ventilation, soon create a heavy, sleepy atmosphere – the very reverse of that required. However, if the only way of improving the atmosphere is to open the windows or doors to the possible distraction of outside noise, this could prove to be just as irritating. There may be little that you can do to correct these ills on the day of the meeting so such possibilities should influence your choice of room.

A similar environmental limitation may be imposed by lighting. If there is any possibility of needing to use any kind of projector or television, it may be necessary to darken the room. Is this possible? Are there curtains or blinds and, even if there are, how effective are they? In particular, check that no stray bands of light fall across the screen (taking care that you check this at about the same time of day as that intended for your meeting).

The nature of the room lights and their control should also be considered. Fluorescent lighting is widely used as it is bright and cost-effective but, for the purposes of a presentation, any need to lower the lights will require an abrupt change rather than a more gentle dimming. Different presenters may also be tempted to experiment with various lighting arrangements during their presentations – causing a significant interruption and distraction. If your organisation is to devote a considerable time to formal presentations, a variable control of the lights would be a worthwhile investment.

Room 'decoration' is another consideration. If the room is to be used as something of a showpiece, there may be an understandable temptation to turn it into a gallery for your products. Resist the temptation. Any such exhibits, captioned photographs or advertisements will be silent conspirators in a plot to distract attention from your speakers. This is not fair to them and weakens your own purpose.

For a meeting involving a largish number of visitors, where will they leave their coats (and briefcases if a site tour is planned)? The availability of an adjacent, lockable room to act as cloakroom should help to avoid a troublesome clutter in the main room (and preferably supplied with one or more cloakroom racks of coat hangers).

Wherever the meeting or presentation is to take place, you should ensure *privacy* and avoid interruptions which impair progress and imply a lack of importance for the meeting or presentation subject. This is obviously a particular danger if you choose to use an office so you should make a point of re-directing phone calls and ensuring that your most frequent internal contacts know that you will be unavailable.

Seating Arrangements

Formal, Routine, Minuted Meeting
Most formal meetings are held with people sat around a table with a chairman sat at the head of the table. This convention immediately recognises a position of power at one end of the table and, not surprisingly, there is a similar 'power position' at the other end. This is not merely a reflection of tradition but of

the view afforded uniquely to those at the ends of a long rectangular table.

The only other locations which allow the whole table to be swept at a glance without moving the head through more than a right angle are the corner locations. For this reason, these positions are also to be favoured by those wanting to influence a meeting.

If you, as meeting organiser, want to extend your influence yet further, you should consider the effect of *assigned seating*. For example, if you believe that a number of those attending are likely to share similar views, there would be a lot of sense in splitting them up so that they cannot readily give the impression of a powerful – and, therefore influential – block during the meeting. If you try to anticipate the attitudes to an issue of those attending, the most balanced arrangement would alternate attitudes in much the way that men and women are generally alternated around a dinner table. However, in an international meeting, there would obviously be no point in alternating those using different languages!

Problem Solving Meeting
This is likely to benefit from the active and equal involvement of all present – particularly during brainstorming. This is not promoted by the long rectangular table common to formal meetings as those in the middle can, if they choose, contribute little.

A more suitable arrangement for the even-handedness demanded of brainstorming is to seat people in a circle. This immediately places everybody on a par but the arrangement does suffer from the difficulty of using a flip chart. If a flip chart (or similar focus) has to be used in the meeting, this should obviously be visible to all. This can be achieved, together with a continued balance between those present, if chairs are arranged in a 'U'.

Training
By its nature, training demands significant interaction between trainer and trainees and so the 'U' arrangement of chairs with the trainer being at the 'focus' of the 'U' is very suitable. Certainly, the rectangular table is inappropriate – as, in most

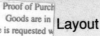

cases ... om layout with chairs (and tables)
place ...

La... ly influenced by the nature of any
train... onse. If, for example, the training
is to ... npetitive team events, each team
shou... le – but, if possible, still attempting ... benefits of the 'U' structure for
plen...

Pres...

In v... of an overhead screen, this must
prov... ntion for the audience. Indeed, the
nee... tion to be switched, at the will of
the ... f and the screen is likely to be the
dete... ayout requiring all in the audience
to b... al direction with equal ease.

... cing of the screen has already been
adv... isual aids and this is one possibility
of ... strated below where consideration
has ... ossible demands of additional aids
which, although helpful, complicate room layout.

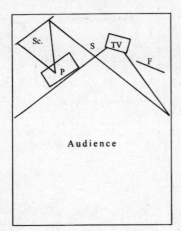

Arranged for a right-handed speaker,
this room layout accommodates:

P- Overhead projector

Sc. - Screen

TV - Video and television

F - Flip chart

and, of course, the speaker - S.

For a left-handed speaker, the layout
should be mirrored about a vertical line
down the room centre.

Wherever multiple facilities are brought into play, you must be able to switch from one to the other with the minimum of delay and disruption. If this cannot be achieved, you must seriously consider forgoing one or more aids in the interests of presentation coherence and continuity.

The speaker's location in the diagram positions him such that he does not obstruct the field of view of any of the audience for either the screen or the television and so can comment on either and even point out details. However, when neither is in use, he can move and approach the audience or move to the flip chart without causing a disturbance.

Audience seating for this general room layout will depend upon the purpose of the meeting – as already discussed – but is not limited other than having to remain within the lines showing the limits of their fields of view for the facilities to be used.

This is a good, general purpose arrangement but the addition of either a 35mm projector or a computer terminal (to be used by the speaker) adds complications that urge the removal of at least one of the more familiar facilities.

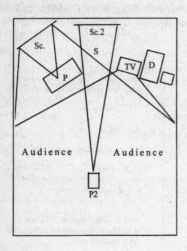

Arranged for a right-handed speaker, this room layout accommodates:

P - Overhead projector

Sc. - Screen

TV - Video and television

     Plus

P2 - a 35mm projector

Sc. 2 - a second screen

D - a desk for a computer keyboard.

Messy isn't it?

Even as sketched above, the arrangement is far from ideal for the range of 'aids' as the position shown for the television will obstruct part of the second screen for the extreme right section of the audience.

But why the second screen? This is necessary if you are to avoid a rather unsatisfactory compromise. The overhead projector is, necessarily, close to its screen and so the screen itself should be angled down toward the projector (which needs to be low to prevent its angled mirror irritating part of the audience). By contrast, the 35mm projector is likely to be much further away and so will require a vertical screen. (Indeed, the projector position shown – in the middle of the audience – is far from ideal as cables may be vulnerable even if taped down. A better position would be hard against the rear wall.) An alternative that might be worth considering would place the 35mm projector right next to the overhead projector and angled to the same screen. This would simplify the room layout but the projected slides would be rather small.

A yet better alternative emphasises the versatility of the LCD panel. Although this was treated with some reserve in Chapter 4, if the alternative to its use is the confusion of hardware seen above, it offers a major improvement. 35mm photographs can be transferred to a computer disk and projected onto the first screen. This totally overcomes the irritating need both for the second screen and the 35mm projector vulnerably located in the audience. Furthermore, the television can also be removed as any video can also be shown at large scale on the first screen by feeding the video signal to the LCD panel. The resulting arrangement is a vast improvement.

After deciding the arrangement of the facilities, a final consideration is how to lay out their various power and control cables. This is particularly important as, if any of your guests should trip, this could be both embarrassing and disruptive. Consequently, if at all possible, all cables should be restricted to the presenter's end of the room where the more limited 'traffic' will reduce the risk of a mishap. Even then, however, all cables should be taped to the floor so that no presenter suffers the misfortune of providing some unintended entertainment! Excess cable length should be coiled in true naval style and taped beneath the projector table. This is not only neater, it will prevent any possibility of snaring a delegate – or your reputation for customer care!

If any cable *has* to be run through the audience's region, it should be laid beneath chairs as well as being taped to the floor.

**The important thing is to think of these possibilities in advance and
sketch them out rather than shuffling furniture – or, worse, accepting a bad room arrangement without appreciating the possible consequences!**

Room Layout – Summary

Decide the **purpose** of your meeting and select a **suitable room**. Consider size, quality, decoration, lighting and privacy.

Arrange **seating to suit the purpose** – committee, problem-solving, training or seminar.

Locate hardware with care and consideration so that it can be used without disrupting the flow of the meeting and the entire audience can see and hear without distractions or obstructions.

Tape down cables to minimise the risk of accidents.

10

Organising A Seminar

Once you have seen the benefits that can result from an effective presentation, you are likely to want to draw on their potential with greater frequency. Organising a seminar will become an attractive temptation but should only be pursued if you are prepared for the work necessary to make it a success. Like any presentation, it has the potential either to enhance or to damage reputations.

A seminar sets logistical problems and demands organisational skills, patience – and, at times – a sorely tested sense of humour. However, two major factors, in common with the skills required for making an effective presentation, are the needs to prepare thoroughly and to think of the audience. Indeed, if you are the main organiser of the seminar, your customers not only include the audience but also the several speakers who will contribute to the event. You will, perhaps, have to coax, encourage and look after your stars so that they contribute to the success that you all want.

But, to begin at the beginning, let's call in Kipling's Honest Serving Men again to help focus our thoughts.

What?
What do you want to achieve? A seminar can have a very wide range of purposes and, as with any effective presentation, you are far more likely to achieve your purpose if you have identified your objectives clearly and have communicated them effectively to all the contributors. Is it to be an internal training course, a sales drive or an exchange of current thinking between

experts? Is it likely to be relaxed and friendly or controversial and, perhaps, heated? If the latter, how will you and your organisation benefit?

Whatever the declared aim, you are surely – and not unreasonably – hoping for some kudos as a result of your efforts. This will be your reward for *attention to detail* in anticipating and preparing to satisfy the needs of your speakers and your guests. Delegates remember a seminar long after it is over for the little things that either pleased or frustrated them. Was it possible to make and receive phone calls easily? Was there somewhere to leave a coat without it simply adding to a jumble sale pile? These points must be right if, in the eyes and memories of many delegates, you are to graduate to being judged on the true merit of the event.

A thorough answer to this first 'What' will help considerably in answering the second: what should be featured in the seminar programme?

A valuable contributor to success is to arrange a varied programme which does not require your guests to endure a Marathon of talks but also offers the opportunity to participate, to walk around and observe activities and to meet with both the presenters and their fellow guests in informal circumstances. This will ease the heavy demands upon concentration, will help the presenters to maintain attention during their talks and will be rewarded by your guests carrying away happy – and satisfied – memories.

But, for the talks themselves, you will still need to think carefully about their content and sequence. If you really want to introduce relatively advanced concepts to a largely non-expert audience, you must programme a suitable talk to establish the basics well before any more demanding topics are attempted.

Who?
There are two obvious questions posed by 'Who': who would you like to attend and who should be invited or encouraged to speak?

The answer to the first question will flow naturally from the clear identification of the purpose of your seminar. If the seminar is part of a sales drive, you will surely need to attract a sufficient number of influential customers? If you want the seminar to carry some weight among experts, it must attract experts – both in the audience and as speakers.

The second 'Who' is a little more sensitive. Your presenters will need to have a comfortable familiarity with their subjects but, as you must know, this is an insufficient qualification in itself. Each speaker must also have the additional skill to be able to interest or, better still, to enthuse an audience. And, of course, they must *want* to contribute.

Prepare a list of possible names, those whom you know to have the necessary subject knowledge and then, in an adjacent column, identify those whom, from your own experience or by reputation, you know to be effective presenters. It would be wise to enlist assistance from a number of colleagues to arrive at a list that minimises your inevitable personal bias.

Between you, you should be able to devise an initial list of suitable targets. But why should they choose to contribute? What will they get from it?

It is now time to meet 'Why'.

Why?

Why should your potential presenters agree to contribute to your seminar? The very fact that they have been selected implies that they are busy people with plenty of calls on their time so why should they choose to do you a favour?

If the event is an internal seminar, you may, of course, be able to instruct rather than request but it would surely be much better if every contributor genuinely wanted to be involved?

One powerful incentive for the extrovert and ambitious is that such events offer them a stage to demonstrate their skills and understanding; indeed, you may receive some unwanted volunteers for this very reason. More often, however, inexperienced presenters may require some sympathetic coaxing to persuade them to contribute. In such cases, take every precaution to ensure that the overall presentation is of the standard that all involved would want. Assist them with constructive criticism and rehearsals in order to build up their confidence and skills.

As for the potential delegates, why should anybody choose to attend your seminar, thereby sacrificing the time that they would otherwise devote to many other things? They must be persuaded to believe that they will benefit in a way that would not otherwise be readily possible. In effect, to use a marketing term, you have to offer a 'unique selling point'. But as each individual is, well, individual, you cannot hope to attract the range of people that you would like to attend with just one piece of bait.

Once again, you must consider the likely interests of your potential audience and prepare a programme that will contain a wide range of attractions. Such considerations should help you to prepare an interesting and varied seminar programme but, if the event is to last more than one day, you should also consider offering some optional free-time entertainment. It might also be helpful to devise an entertainment programme for any partners of seminar delegates. After all, they may be visiting a strange place and would welcome friendly assistance. At the very least, the fact that you have taken the trouble to offer such a service should ingratiate you with your guests. Isn't this likely to help in breaking down any barriers between you and so help you to approach your intended objective?

How?

But even if potential delegates are themselves attracted by your programme and by the optional extra-curricular activities, they are still likely to have to justify the visit to their boss. Indeed, a comprehensive entertainment package might make many a boss suspicious! Another 'How?' might be persuasive, provided the answer to 'how much?' is acceptable. But if a decision to attend reduces to mere money, you have probably failed to devise the right programme for the targeted delegate.

Your programme will have to be increasingly appealing as the travelling distance required for the delegate increases. Given the heavy demands on time, every extra day required away from the delegate's home office weighs against attendance. Consequently, this problem should be eased by responding to 'When' only after very careful thought.

When?

Fixing a Date
Selecting the right time for a seminar might make all the difference between success and failure – particularly if you

hope to attract delegates from far afield. In such circumstances, even a well thought-out programme may be insufficient to persuade a sufficient number to commit time to travelling great distances in addition to the time at the seminar. However, far more will be tempted if the time demanded merely *extends* their other commitments. Consequently, review the forthcoming events for your particular industry or activity for at least the year ahead. If there are to be any international meetings or exhibitions in your country that are likely to attract your targeted delegates, schedule your seminar for adjacent days (preferably *after* so that your guests will overcome jet-lag during the earlier event). If they choose to attend the larger event, their travel time and costs will already have been justified and so you will only have to persuade them – and their bosses – to add a few days. This extra justification for travelling so far is likely to be welcomed.

Another timing consideration might be imposed if you hope to attract delegates from Moslem countries. The month-long Ramadan is a period of fasting that requires believers to forgo eating during daylight hours so it could be embarrassing if half your delegates are over-faced with food while others are gently sipping water! Unfortunately, as the Moslem calendar is based on the lunar month, Ramadan does not occur at the same time every year in the Christian calendar: you will have to check when it is due.

'When' poses at least two further important questions: when should you start planning the event and, during the seminar, when should the various talks be programmed?

Starting to Plan
Think of your own and your colleagues' commitments. Your diaries may well be heavily committed for at least the next month and this time stretches further into the future with the seniority of the person. So, if you would welcome the presence of royalty, you had better start planning at least a year in advance.

Distance also weighs on the planning schedule. If significant travel has to be justified, you must allow time for your targeted delegates to obtain the agreement of their bosses – who will

have numerous other demands contending for attention. Allowing a month for such steady diplomacy, at least another month
should be allowed for each remote delegate to organise a more
comprehensive itinerary in which your seminar is but a part and,
possibly, to obtain necessary visas. And, ideally, you would
surely want to be confident of a reasonable attendance before
your potential contributors have spent considerable time in
preparing their presentations? Indeed, a healthy guest list may
well be a powerful persuader to obtain willing contributors. You
therefore need a reasonable number of delegate commitments in
sufficient time to allow contributors to fit their preparatory work
into their busy schedules. This pushes the necessary start of
planning back at least six months before the intended seminar
date.

The Seminar Programme
You have already identified attractive and interesting talks and
events for your seminar but their overall impact will be all the
greater if they are arranged into a mutually supportive sequence.
The possible need to place introductory talks early in the programme has already been noted but great benefits will also come
from varying the style as well as the content of the programme.
Consequently, try not to string too many talks into an attention-
sapping procession but intersperse them with interludes of a
different nature – if only a coffee break.

Another aid to maintaining attention – if a little gimmicky – is
to organise a quiz which will test the recall of delegates for the
various talks. This should not, however, be in any way threatening or reminiscent of a school test (with detention for the
failures). Rather, it should be presented as a bit of fun with some
small prize to be presented to the best performer. Announced at
the start of the seminar, this should add a small incentive to
maintain attention through the 'stickier bits'.

More effective in maintaining genuine attention is to alternate
each spoken presentation with various audience activities that
engage their interest and involvement. For example, the dreaded
after lunch slot would be better filled by, say, a tour of inspection
of the factory or offices – anything that gets the delegates moving
again after what might have been an over-satisfying lunch! This

consideration is a major influence for answering the final question: 'Where'.

Where?
The simple answer to this question – especially if you are organising your first seminar – is on home ground. You need to be in control during the seminar so introducing the added complication of a 'foreign' venue is not recommended. 'Playing at home' offers the advantages of knowing exactly what facilities are available and whom to approach in order to obtain them, should they be necessary in the event of unforeseen circumstances or unusual delegate requirements. A 'home' venue can also add the variety of 'walkabouts' and, if you intend to show off your technology or methods, this is immediately available 'live' without having to rely on impersonal photographs or videos. Additional room space at no extra cost and little inconvenience can also probably be arranged, if required. Furthermore, you will have access to the intended seminar room or rooms well in advance of the event and can rearrange it to suit your own needs: in short, you will be in control – a very comforting feeling.

However, there may be very sound reasons for planning the seminar away from home – either in a convenient local hotel or even in a completely different location or country. In this event, you should consider alternative venues very carefully so that the facilities offered will match your needs as closely as possible (and these needs will be considerable as we shall shortly see).

Inspect what is on offer if at all possible or, if not, ensure that a very reliable local agent, armed with a very clear list of your requirements, does so on your behalf. In any event, provide the hotel or remote site with a written specification of your needs and obtain their confirmation that they will conform – along with their price quotation – so that there can be no doubt as to who is doing what. This specification should include an adequate allowance for both preparing the room and clearing up again afterwards. Table and chair arrangements and the location of basic seminar hardware can be defined in advance and, *with agreement*, set out by the local staff but you will feel considerably more comfortable if you allow sufficient time to satisfy yourself that important little details like trailing leads are dealt with. You will want to confirm and, if necessary, adjust these arrangements for yourself without your delegates arriving at the same time!

An additional complication for any overseas seminar is that the technical specifications for any hardware requirements are likely to be different. In particular, the local power supply may not match the home standard either for voltage or frequency. Furthermore, should you intend to use any video, this may have to be converted into the local standard.

The Pal system is used in the UK and in many other European and Asian countries but there is no neat geographical distribution of this standard. France uses Secam and many other countries – often with French links – also use this standard. Pal and Secam are not entirely incompatible but colour will be lost if the video recording does not match the playback equipment.

NTSC, largely associated with the USA and other continental American countries, is not so tolerant of Pal or Secam tapes. It is possible to find multiple standard equipment that will play one tape on a television designed for the other standard but, in the absence of this luxury, the only recourse is to arrange for the tape to be converted.

Even simple things like the design of electrical plugs may prove to be a time-consuming frustration if you hope to use your own equipment so check these essentials with a reliable local agent in good time.

The Vital Details

By this point, you will have developed a much clearer picture of what your seminar is intended to be but there are many additional considerations if you are to achieve success. How will the delegates travel? Do they know how to find your factory, office or chosen venue? Will they be able to park? How will they be fed? Where will they stay if the seminar is to span more than one day or guests from afar are expected? A comprehensive checklist will be found later in this chapter but this should not be used as an excuse for not thinking about the specific needs of *your* seminar. However, some details are of such importance that they are reviewed in greater detail below.

Catering

For any seminar planned to last more than a few hours, delegates will expect to be fed. Can you rely on your own catering facilities for this extra demand or should you employ contract caterers? And what should be on the menu? Some of your guests may have dietary restrictions for reasons of health, religion or simple conviction and you can establish your intention of attending to their needs by querying any such restrictions in your written invitation. What is on offer should enable anybody to eat adequately without having to compromise their normal practice.

A buffet lunch is an ideal option for mid-day for several reasons. Individual choices can be made with ease (using simple labels to identify possibly sensitive ingredients) and people can circulate while eating to establish informal links with other delegates and speakers. However, do ensure that the room or rooms set aside for the buffet are well arranged so that congestion at doorways and at the buffet table is reduced to a minimum. In particular, the bar should be as far away as possible from the entrance door in order to draw visitors into the room. Promote a one-way flow and offer suitable seating away from the buffet to encourage the full use of the available space rather than a pile-up around the food table. You should be able to leave these matters to the caterers but agreeing such plans in advance might avoid possible confusion on the day.

Evening entertainment is more likely to involve a seated meal. The same dietary concerns obviously affect the choice of menu but you now also have to give thought to seating arrangements. Do you assign the seating in advance or allow your guests to sort themselves out? Each has its advantages and drawbacks. For any assigned seating arrangement, you run the risk of giving offence by placing some delegates – in their eyes – carelessly. Additionally, many delegates may want to pursue discussions that they have already struck up and so may be frustrated by the enforced separation. However, if you simply leave it to chance, there is the risk that distinctly odd combinations may occur which hinder or prevent healthy conversation. A tolerable compromise is to enlist the support of sufficient colleagues to look after particular guests with similar interests and – obviously – the same languages!

Communications
This need has been mentioned briefly but it bears repeating more fully. Some delegates may welcome the freedom of being able to get away from their home office but many will feel uneasy at their absence and will want both to make and receive calls with some frequency. This need should be anticipated and adequate telephone facilities should be both available and made known to your guests almost as they arrive.

Overseas visitors may also welcome assistance to organise their onward travel. If this is overlooked, it would not be surprising if such delegates fail to give the seminar the attention that it might otherwise deserve.

Hardware
The above details concentrate upon the needs of the delegates but, as seminar organiser, you must be at least as concerned with the well-being of your presenters. Their agreement to participate should include a clear mutual understanding of exactly *what* they will be contributing so that you can fit this into your programme at a suitable point. But *how* will they make their presentation? Will they use an overhead or 35mm projector? Will they use a short video? Will they bring any hardware items of their own? You must establish these needs well in advance and ensure that the necessary equipment is readily available. The last thing you want is disruption and delay between presentations.

Everything Else
There is a very long list of other details that have to be organised in advance of a successful seminar. A suggested list appears below but, before looking at it, try preparing your own. The effort of thinking it through will help to organise your thoughts and there may be some special or additional needs for your seminar that are not listed.

Try to think of and arrange your list in a chronological sequence so that it will eventually provide you with a scheduled checklist. Once completed, the steady ticking off of completed tasks will lend confidence that all will be well for the event itself.

Purpose defined
Date fixed
Contributors invited
Contributors agreed
Venue chosen and booked
Guests invited (with seminar programme, programme of extra-curricular events, route map, local hotels, as required)
Additional hardware requirements identified and, if necessary, hired
Guest list confirmed
Room layout established
Catering organised and buffet room(s) booked and layout planned
Additional glasses etc. hired if required
Executive coach hired (if collecting from a central point and for local transport during an extended seminar)
Flowers ordered
Assistance for coffee and tea breaks obtained
Site tour guides organised
Secretarial services arranged
Cloakroom arrangements in place
Written papers received from contributors
Document dossier ordered
Photographer arranged
Hotel bookings confirmed for delegates
Identification badges ordered
Necessary safety equipment available in sufficient quantity
Document dossier assembled
Reception and all seminar rooms cleaned for use
Room layout completed with all hardware in place and working correctly
Flowers in place
Contributors familiar with room lighting switches and equipment operation as required
Site security made aware of visit
All staff aware of seminar
'Thank you' gifts obtained for seminar helpers
Site flags flying

Anything else? If you are planning an overseas seminar, you

obviously need to add to this list the special preparations for travel – injections, passports in order, visas, tickets, hotel and hire car bookings.

Well, did you add anything to the list? As you can see, numerous factors might affect the success of your seminar and so you must be meticulous in your planning well before the opening day if you are to have a good chance of achieving your objectives. Even then, you will need to be attentive and responsive to circumstances as they develop during the event itself. However, by this time you will have received the full commitment and attention of all those who have agreed to help and so you will not be alone in working to ensure success.

Practise

This review has attempted to consider the needs of quite a large seminar and so several aspects may be unnecessary for your seminar. Indeed, it would be foolish to be too ambitious for a first attempt as any failure would be very public and, potentially, very embarrassing. Consequently, as with all other aspects of presentation, seek opportunities to hone your skills in less trying and less significant circumstances. For example, you could use a similar approach to plan a dinner party or family celebration. Indeed, a children's party might be every bit as taxing as a full blooded seminar!

Whatever opportunity you pursue, plan it out in detail and, after the event, analyse how things went. Did you forget anything? What went wrong? What was particularly successful? Prepare a simple questionnaire and ask your guests for their opinions and suggestions for improvement. But make sure that this is more than just an empty ritual. Ask 'closed' questions which require no more than a tick in a numbered box. This demands less of each delegate and vastly eases the important task of analysis.

Ensure that the questions really help the improvement process. Questions like 'Did you enjoy the seminar?' may obtain a flattering response but will this be helpful? It will be more useful to gauge delegate opinion of the length and complexity of each talk or the effectiveness of visual aids (too many/too few, too simple/ too busy). Really use the experience to improve for next time. Your colleagues and your company will admire and thank you.

Organising a Seminar – Summary
Obtain the help of 'Kipling's six honest serving men'.

> **What** is the purpose of the seminar? What do you want to achieve?
> **Who** is to attend? Who is to speak?
> **Why** should they come?
> **How** much will it cost?
> **When** should it be scheduled and when should you start planning?
> **Where** should it be held? A 'home' setting offers many advantages but, if using a remote location, ensure that you make *detailed* arrangements for all necessary facilities establishing a clear understanding of responsibilities.

Attend to the **vital details** – catering, communications and hardware.

Prepare and work through a **comprehensive checklist**.

After the event, **review** your successes and failures so as to improve for the future.

11

Continuous Improvement

I hope that you have found this book to be interesting and valuable. But, of course, simply reading any guide is not the same as *being there*. Consequently, to become a really effective presenter, you must take every opportunity to stand up and speak. Every such occasion offers a small step to improvement and you should ensure that you make the most of every chance.

If you have attended any seminar or training function in recent years, you have surely been asked to complete an appraisal questionnaire after the event? This is a formal recognition of the value of continuous improvement and a simple attempt to respond to the need. Perhaps you have been able to benefit personally from such feedback? But don't rely on just this to improve further; there are numerous ways in which you can improve and, if you pursue them all, you can give yourself the pleasure of *knowing* that you're improving – and, on occasions, be entertained by the process into the bargain! This final chapter offers some suggestions for encouraging and monitoring your progress.

Do It!
As already stated, if you are to improve, there is no substitute for doing it – no matter what the activity. But, when concentrating on presentation, there may be little attention left for critical self-appraisal and so faults may go undetected and grow strong through habit. You therefore need to encourage constructive criticism from co-operative members of your audience, colleagues perhaps.

But can you be sure that they are being wholly honest when they say 'Great'? How often does any colleague really offer constructive criticism? A lack of criticism does not mean wholesale approval but, generally, reflects an understandable reluctance to criticise – especially of an unpopular activity. Unless you *know* – from spontaneous audience reaction – that you've done well, you are likely to be unconvinced by plaudits from your colleagues.

So, what alternatives are available?

Train

There are numerous training courses available to help improve speaking skills. They are likely to make very similar recommendations to those in this book but, unlike a book, they also offer the opportunity to develop skills through practice in a safe – but constructively critical – environment. Faults will be pointed out but with recommendations for improvement. If you respond appropriately, you should be able to make significant progress within just a matter of days. This, in turn, will improve your confidence and will add further to your effectiveness as a presenter.

So, take advantage of a training course: it will help you over the initial and most daunting obstacles to effective presentation.

Self-criticism

When aware of your faults, you are likely to be harder on yourself than anybody else and so, *used constructively*, self-criticism can be a very effective driver of improvement. But it may be difficult to focus any attention on self-criticism while sweating in the spotlight of the presentation itself. Consequently, you must make the most of the time before and after your presentation.

When preparing, take the time to criticise your work from the imagined viewpoint of the audience. Can they really be expected to understand that phrase or technical term? Is that overhead as clear as it could be? Record and listen to your rehearsal. Are you talking too quickly? Do you throw in redundant words like a parrot? Are there too many pointless pauses or are you talking too quietly?

These last two points can be mercilessly revealed by the use of a simple dictation machine which is programmed to switch off after more than about four seconds of 'silence'. Switch on the machine at the remotest point in the room and then see if you can keep it going so that the playback does not feature the give-away whine of automatic starts!

After your presentation, don't just slump into a thankful lethargy for having survived the ordeal! Give yourself a figurative pat on the back by all means but then review your presentation while it is still fresh in your mind.

This is an interesting test in itself. Can you remember anything about the event – or had you been speaking from another world? Can you remember looking at the audience? What did you see: smiles, attentive faces or drooping eyes and yawns? Whichever it was – if you can remember – why did they react that way? What, in your presentation, was effective at exciting genuine attention and what acted like a drug? Learn the lessons for future presentations: remember the winning formula but ensure that you never repeat a gaffe.

Some seminars – and many training events – are recorded on video. This provides you with an ideal opportunity to learn from your own mistakes. Make sure that you get a copy of the tape and, torture though it may be at first, be honest in identifying your strengths and weaknesses. You owe it to yourself – and to your future audiences.

As you watch the recording, remember what you should be doing and – more importantly, perhaps – what you shouldn't. Are you maintaining effective contact with your audience with your eyes – without staring at just one sympathetic character? Do you turn to talk to the screen when using the overhead projector? Do you move around aimlessly? Are you irritated by your own habitual mannerisms?

These last two can be dramatically exposed by playing the video at high speed. Movements adopt a staccato intensity which is unmistakable and the worst features of your style shout at you soundlessly!

But, if this should be your experience, don't let it upset you. Awareness of a fault is the first – and essential – step to its correction.

Criticise Others
Self-criticism, though a powerful driver for improvement, can often be a painful experience. Criticising others, however, can also be a valuable aid to learning and is certainly less stressful!

I am not advocating telling every other speaker how to perform. Rather, when anybody else is making a presentation, attend carefully not only to what they say but *how* they say it. Look, too, at the audience. How are they reacting? If the presenter is really effective, you may be able to borrow the techniques to improve your own performance. By contrast – and, perhaps, sadly more likely – you will be able to recognise the consequences of errors and this should strengthen your resolve to avoid similar faults. In any event, the exercise should provide you with a form of 'entertainment' even during the most boring of presentations. Furthermore, if the speaker should request criticism, you will be able to respond with genuinely helpful observations instead of useless platitudes.

Learn From the Pros
If we could all learn by example there should be no excuse for poor presentation skills. We are bombarded by the media every day but, in general, the radio and television presenters are so flawless that we take their skills for granted without really observing them.

Certainly, a thoughtful consideration of how radio and television presenters perform offers a tremendous fund of improvement tips. The snag is that their skills are deployed so effortlessly, and the result is seemingly so natural, that we usually fail to recognise or benefit from the learning opportunities. As an apprentice presenter yourself, you should take full advantage of the learning opportunities offered by the masters every day.

When they speak, how often can you count an 'umm'? True, from programmes like 'It'll be alright on the night', we know that even the professionals occasionally need several 'takes' to get it right – but doesn't this stress the importance of preparation and rehearsal?

Have you noticed that if an interviewee introduces some three letter acronym or jargon term, the thoughtful professional interviewer will either 'translate' or immediately ask for the explanation. Consideration of the audience must always be uppermost in the presenter's thoughts.

And how could you fail to be impressed by their timing? Admittedly, they have a producer keeping them to the pro- gramme schedule but I still find the split-second 'fit' with the time signal to be smoothly professional – almost always. How often do business meetings even start with such punctuality, let alone finish as scheduled? But such discipline is a major help to focusing talk and discussion and, if it's known that timing will be strict, it demands a careful preparation and effective use of every available minute.

When television interviewers talk to their guests, where do they look? And when talking to you, the viewer, have you noticed how odd it seems when, on rare occasions, they pick the wrong camera? But where do *you* look when talking to an audience? And, when in a meeting around a table, how do you ensure that all present are aware of your concern for their attention? Look at them and ensure that all present are aware of your focus on them.

These same interviewers, when listening, do *they* look away or doodle?

Learning from the professionals can be embarrassing can't it?

What about those occasions when a television presenter leaves the chair to walk about the studio or street: is it aimless wandering? No, there is invariably a purpose. The movement is used to find a new interviewee, to transfer your attention to an exhibit or, perhaps, to a new guest.

And what about those doyens of the projected screen, the weather people? When describing the weather situation, do they look away from you to admire the map? No, they glance at it and sweep a hand to the specific area being described but they continue to talk to you, not to the map. But, equally, they do not ignore the map in order to describe the situation, they use it to amplify what they say. They call up the next relevant weather situation, describe it and then move smoothly to the next. No chart is screened before its spoken cue and none is kept beyond its need. Isn't this the way to use visual aids?

Ideas for the effective preparation of visual aids are also

abundantly available in the media. The pages of the financial press, in particular, carry charts and graphs that are designed to convey their essential message with maximum impact and minimum risk of confusion. However, press graphics invariably have to feature short captions or explanations as there is no voice to carry the message. In a presentation, these captions should not feature on the graphic as they would be a complicating distraction. Rather, they should form the outline for your spoken interpretation of the picture.

This is clearly seen when television news and current affairs programmes use graphics to drive home a point. Any words only appear *as they are spoken* and graphics rarely contain even as many as twenty words unless reporting a direct quotation.

What about dress and stance? Are they careless, rumpled or casual? No, both are always *appropriate*. Studio presenters are always immaculately dressed and always sit or stand with an attentive manner. Even war zone reporters dress for the occasion. This is, no doubt, primarily for comfort and safety but the very appropriateness of their clothing and their evident attention to the situation strengthens their spoken message.

But even the pros are fallible and it can be both entertaining and instructive to listen and watch questioningly and critically. Why did he turn then? Where is she going? Was that a sensible move? How do they do that? More importantly, how can *I* do that?

You *can* do that. All it takes is persistence and a readiness to learn from every opportunity. Let's see if you're prepared to do it.

Consider the various situations in which presentation skills might be useful to you: for example, discussing some opportunity with one or more of your colleagues or staff, explaining to a customer, negotiating with a supplier, listening to a problem being described. Don't limit yourself to just these examples; make your own list. Think also of the various traits that are valuable in effective presentation: audience rapport, eye contact, vocal expression, stance, body language. Add these to your list so that you have at least a dozen situations or skills.

Now, considering each in turn, in what type of radio or television programme might you expect to find techniques that might be useful in that situation or to illustrate the use of that skill? Pursuing the earlier example, a current affairs debate should be useful in helping discussion skills (not to mention chairmanship); lessons in explaining new ideas or products will surely be found in any science, technology or nature programme. The effective presentation of data should be demonstrated by any programme with a financial angle – even the average news broadcast. Use your imagination to link programmes to learning opportunities and then look and listen critically, not passively. Experiment in applying these techniques yourself at the earliest opportunity.

Progressing in this way, you will *enjoy* developing your presentation skills and, what's more, your audiences will enjoy and respond positively to your presentations. You will become that rare being: an *effective* presenter.

Index

A

Appraisal questionnaire, 116-117, 118
Attention, maintaining, 78-79
Audience, consideration of the, 12, 20-21
, involving the, 79,80
understanding, 8-9

B

Bad news, conveying, 93-94
Body language, 12-13, 87

C

Cables, placing of, 104
Catering, 113
Cloakroom, 99
Clothes, 70, 123
Computers, 43
Confidence, 9, 13, 64 *et seq.*
Conviction, 13
Criticism, constructive, 66-67, 118-119, 121
, self-, 65, 119-120

D

Data handling, 45 *et seq.*
(see also symbols)
Decoration of room, 99

Demonstrations, 42-43
Detail, attention to, 13
Dress (see clothes)

E

English, command of, 13
Entertaining, 79-80
Enthusiasm, 14
Essential message (see message)
Exhibitions, 42-43
Experience, 14
Eyes, 76-77
(see also facial expression)

F

Facial expression, 77, 87
Facts, marshalling, 22
Finishing, 24
Flip charts, 30, 31, 32-33
Framework, logical, 22

G

Graphs, 49-58

H

Hand-outs, 81-82
Hands, use of, 77-78
Histogram, 60-62
Humour, 14, 81

I
Integrity, 14-15, 81
Interruptions, 81
   , avoid, 99

J
Jargon, 13, 20, 66
Job interview, 87-88

K
Knowledge, 15

L
Lighting, 41, 98-99
Listening, active, 86-87

M
Media interviews, 94-95
Message, essential, 21-22

N
Negotiation, 89-93
Nerves, 67-68, 70, 71
Notes, 25-28

O
Objective, 21
Overheads, 30, 31, 33-40

P
Passion, 15
Positive thinking, 67-68
Power supply, foreign, 112
Preparation, 8, 9, 15, 18 *et seq.*,
   67, 68-70, 119
   time, 19
Presentations, large theatre,
   93-94
   , small theatre, 85-87
Professional presenters, 121-124
Props (see visual aids)
Public speaking, 84 *et seq.*

Q
Questions, 80-81

R
Rehearsal, 69-70, 119-120
Research, need for, 19-20
Room layout, 10, 97 *et seq.*
   , studying the, 68-69

S
Sales pitch, small scale, 87-88
   (see also negotiation)
Seating arrangements, 85-86,
   97-98, 99-104, 113
Seminar, equipment for a, 114
   , fixing dates for a, 108-109
   , overseas, 115-116
   programme, 110-111
   , travel to, 112
   venue, choosing a, 111-112
Series of talks, 21
Slides, 30, 31, 41-42
Sorting ideas, 23-24
Speaking, effective, 7-8, 11 *et
   seq.*
   , facets of, 12-17
Stance, 73-74, 123
Starting, 24, 71
Symbols representing data, 59-60

T
Telephone facilities, 114
Training, 95, 119

V
Venue (see room, studying the)
Video standard, 112
Videos, 30, 31, 42
Visual aids, 8, 25, 29 *et seq.*,
   101-104, 122-123
   , when to use, 30-31
Voice, 15-16, 75-76

RIGHT WAY
PUBLISHING POLICY

HOW WE SELECT TITLES

RIGHT WAY consider carefully every deserving manuscript. Where an author is an authority on his subject but an inexperienced writer, we provide first-class editorial help. The standards we set make sure that every **RIGHT WAY** book is practical, easy to understand, concise, informative and delightful to read. Our specialist artists are skilled at creating simple illustrations which augment the text wherever necessary.

CONSISTENT QUALITY

At every reprint our books are updated where appropriate, giving our authors the opportunity to include new information.

FAST DELIVERY

We sell **RIGHT WAY** books to the best bookshops throughout the world. It may be that your bookseller has run out of stock of a particular title. If so, he can order more from us at any time – we have a fine reputation for "same day" despatch, and we supply any order, however small (even a single copy), to any bookseller who has an account with us. We prefer you to buy from your bookseller, as this reminds him of the strong underlying public demand for **RIGHT WAY** books. Readers who live in remote places, or who are housebound, or whose local bookseller is unco-operative, can order direct from us by post.

FREE

If you would like an up-to-date list of all **RIGHT WAY** titles currently available, please send a stamped self-addressed envelope to

ELLIOT RIGHT WAY BOOKS,
KINGSWOOD, SURREY, KT20 6TD, U.K.